POETRY NOW
NORTHERN ENGLAND 2003

Edited by

Kelly Oliver

First published in Great Britain in 2002 by
POETRY NOW
Remus House,
Coltsfoot Drive,
Peterborough, PE2 9JX
Telephone (01733) 898101
Fax (01733) 313524

All Rights Reserved

Copyright Contributors 2002

HB ISBN 0 75434 383 9
SB ISBN 0 75434 384 7

FOREWORD

Although we are a nation of poets we are accused of not reading poetry, or buying poetry books. After many years of listening to the incessant gripes of poetry publishers, I can only assume that the books they publish, in general, are books that most people do not want to read.

Poetry should not be obscure, introverted, and as cryptic as a crossword puzzle: it is the poet's duty to reach out and embrace the world.

The world owes the poet nothing and we should not be expected to dig and delve into a rambling discourse searching for some inner meaning.

The reason we write poetry (and almost all of us do) is because we want to communicate: an ideal; an idea; or a specific feeling. Poetry is as essential in communication, as a letter; a radio; a telephone, and the main criterion for selecting the poems in this anthology is very simple: they communicate.

CONTENTS

Not So Simple Simon	Doreen Dean	1
One Year On	Barbara Blyth	2
Angel Of Fire And Ice	R Darakshani	3
Autumn Tequila	Nicholas Donaldson	4
One Brief Moment	Donald John Tye	5
The Old City Walls Of Newcastle	Kathleen McGowan	6
Beyond The Summer Sun	Tony Gyimes	8
Dreaming	Irene Rogerson	9
I Count	A S Walton	10
The Uke	Jack Bowden	12
Worth's Thief	Christine M Wilkinson	13
Pride Of Place	Adrian Brett	14
The Children's Dream	R Marr	15
Local College	Patrick Brady	16
My Secret Memories	Sylvia McGregor	17
The Air Show	Neal Wright	18
The Room	G D Wilson	20
Winter Wheat	Richard Leitch	21
The Tinker Girl	Maisie Bell	22
The Toon Army	Gwen Stone	24
A Fraternal Settlement	Heather Charnley	25
Room For Improvement	Christine Wylie	26
My County	Kenneth Copley	28
There's Nowt As True As Yorkshire Folk	Leeanne Shires	30
Endeavour 2002	Anne Aitchison	31
Untitled	Mollie Sanderson	32
Eighteenth Century Lovers	Pauline M Parlour	33
Untitled	M Simpson	34
Thank You	Janine Williams	35
In The Lion's Den	Rachel C Zaino	36
Word Painting	N V Wright	37
Derby Day	Dee Yates	38
My Children's Eyes	Gareth Thorpe	40
Garden	Ailsa McDermid	41
Depression	Anne Dunkerley	42

The Friday Footers	Sylvia A Whitaker	43
The Rhythm Of Love	Catherine Watson	44
Confined	Megan Ward	45
The River Calder	David A Garside	46
Sleepless	Rosalind I Caygill	47
Untitled	John Gill	48
Poppy The Heroine	Patsy Preshaw	50
William's Boots	Daphne Clarke	52
Portrait In Sepia	Elizabeth Rimington	53
The Aftermath Of Separation	Keith Tissington	54
The Reunion	Barbara Buckley	55
What He Did Yesterday	Mary Dearnley	56
Yorkshire	Nancy Walecka	58
Reflection	Sue Lupton	59
A Face From The Past	Molly Ann Kean	60
Holiday Time	A Thornton	61
Wheeldale	Barrie Williams	62
All Mixed Up	Hetty Foster	63
Icara, This Winter	Anna Taylor	64
Cornucopia Corner	Phillip Beverley	67
The Other Me	Mark Wood	68
Sorrow In The Garden	Liz Macauley	69
Freedom Of Thought	Matthew Ayre	70
The Steelmakers	Roy Dickinson	72
The Four Yorkshire Regions	Jane Milthorp	74
Dawn Chorus	Jo Leak	76
Keep Trying	Gordon Barnett	79
A Tyke's Tongue	Gerald Elliott	80
White Plumes In The Sun	J Barker	81
A Poem About Fruit	Barbara Ann Hartley	82
Force Of The Sea	Rachel Harrison	83
Sunset To Sunrise	Margaret M Warkup	84
Bridlington Beach	Maurice Wilkinson	85
Septempber 11th 2001	Pttr Manson-Herrod	86
Nobody Listens	Rolo	87
With Gold	D J Price	88
The Foreman	David Watkins	89

Fragmented City (Bradford's Culture Bid)	Kathleen Mary Scatchard	90
A Piece Of England	Kathleen McBurney	91
Time	Barbara Robson	92
Country Cricket	Barbara Williams	93
Bygones	Constance Vera Dewdney	94
Global Warming! Armageddon?	Bah Kaffir	95
Home Thoughts From Home	Charles Holmes	96
A Visit To Wentworth In March 2002	Lyn Wilkinson	97
Listen To The Silence	Jack Birkhead	98
The Five Seasons	David Parker	99
Welder Am I	Kevin Dixon	100
My 25p Rise	J Mary Kirkland	101
I Look In The Mirror And What Do I See?	Emmie Tann	102
Growing Old	Doreen Yewdall	103
Scarborough Rock	Brian M Wood	104
It's Gorn	G Stanley	105
Nature Play	Margaret Ann Tait	106
WWW Dot Con	Olga M Momcilovic	108
Sergeant Pepper Ends The Empire	Peter Ardern	109
Trash	Karen Cawthorn	110
The Addiction	Karen A Neville	112
Hickory Dickory Dock At Penistone Market Town	Margaret Marsh	114
A Naughty Boy	Victor Brunt	115
Green Valley	Ruth Kavanagh	116
Anno Domini	Marjorie Upson	118
The Sea	E D Stevenson	119
The Master Plan	Barbara Dunning	120
Retirement	Bob T	122
Lunch Alfresco	Pauline Boncey	123
Retirement	Mary Parker	124
Friday Night At Paragon Station	Marie Housam	125
Playing The Cards Given	Bill Warby	126
The Old Mill Town	Disillusioned	127

Summer Afternoon At Otley	Deborah Tuddenham	128
The Flood	Catherine Day	129
Industrial Survival	Malcolm Goat	130
Thoughts	K M Parker	132
Feeding The Pain	M J Chadwick	133
Drugs	K Ainsley	134
Catching Games	Charlie Duffin	136
Summer's Gone	H Matthews	138
One Summer's Day	C F Hauxwell	139
The Prince Of The Lonely Night	Emma Warwick	140
Changing Seasons	Christopoher Philpott	141
Hats	Eveline Weighell	142
Glimpses Of Heaven	Mazard Hunter	143
Silhouettes	Maureen Gilbert	144
A Mother's Farewell	M G Clements	145
When Does Romance End?	David Sim	146
Nickey's Year	Jean Naseby	147
A Housewife's Work Is Never Done	Tracey Ibbotson	148
The Disappearing Loos Of Cleveland	David Burton	149
Off To London	Janet Degnan	150
Family Treasures	Jean Lowe	153
The Good Old Days	Jessica Ruggles	154
Gunpowder, Treason And Plot	David Jasper	156
A Plea For Understanding	Ruth Ockendon Laycock	158
The Stepping Stone Path	G Davies	159
Ritual	Steve Urwin	160
Letting Go	M J Ellerton	161
Daisies	Aitch Brown	162
Memories Of Boyhood	M Newble	164
The Tale Of The Ghost Of White Emma 1993	E D Bowen	166
Summer Fields	Andrea Parker	168
Devotion	Carolyn Horner	169

NOT SO SIMPLE SIMON

As a writer I'd been invited to a school
to help a class of ten year olds.

'Simon has problems. He recognises few words
so can't speak in sentences
and he doesn't like strangers'
his teacher said.

That first day I sat on a chair at the front
and read a story to the class
while Simon, eyes fixed firmly on the floor,
sat as far away from me as possible.

The next day I perched on a desk and he sat close,
so close we could almost touch,
and before I left he silently handed me
a drawing he had done.

The third day he gave me, with a shy half smile,
a story he had dictated to his teacher.

I was moved beyond the words he could not recognise.

The fourth day I handed out copies of my poems
and asked for volunteers to read them aloud.

Simon was angry. Threw them on the floor.
Stamped on them.
*'Want
Can't
Want
Can't'*
he raged.

I knew that I had let him down, and remain haunted
by the child who taught me more
about communication than anyone I have ever met.

Doreen Dean

ONE YEAR ON

One year on, passing time
Memories richer
Thoughts are blessed
One year on.

One year on, pain less numbing
Children's laughter
Garden grows
One year on.

One year on, quiet moments
Treasured love, everlasting
Family circle
One year on.

Barbara Blyth

ANGEL OF FIRE AND ICE

Oh angel, are you from fire or snow . . ?
Oh angel, you are angel, but from fire and ice.
Your beautiful redness is from fire and your gentle
                        whiteness is from snow.
You are burning in the fire and freezing in the snow.
Oh no, you are not burning nor freezing.
Whenever you are burning in your fire, your ice prevents you burning,
And whenever you are freezing in your ice, your
                        fire prevents you freezing.
Oh angel! You have not a second's calmness.
Your habit is to burn and your destiny is to freeze.
You burn to teach the peoples of the world patience and faithfulness.
You freeze to give to humanity the lesson of selflessness and sacrifice.
Oh angel! Burn calmly and freeze bravely.
You are teaching us love, kindness, faithfulness, courage,
                        patience, honesty and strength.
Oh angel of fire and ice!
Be happy in your burning and be strong in your freezing.

R Darakshani

AUTUMN TEQUILA

Only one thing to remember
Is something you should never forget
The picture is a memento
Timeless, priceless.
A distant memory, yet so close
Or a photo taken, an importance
For instance, something
A person of course.
Something to remember
A picture hanging on a wall
Looking up to the tall sky
The object of desire makes a tear fall.
Or a smile on your face
Listening to the voices within
Of a person you remember
Whilst in the autumn rain.
A star up above
The look you remember within their eye
Like a sparkling diamond
Like rain drops from the sky.
New York sunshine
A flight across the ocean
A memento that brings emotion.
In the autumn rain
On an occasion of silence
When a tree leaf is falling
Drinking those raindrop tequilas.

Nicholas Donaldson

ONE BRIEF MOMENT

For one brief moment in time
I held an angel of beauty
From high up in Heaven above
A beautiful angel I long to hold and love
With the whole of my heart and soul
And her sweet angel's name was Diane
Sweet Diane Draper.

Her eyes were emerald green
And sparkled brighter than the stars at night
Her lips were ruby red and sweeter
Far, far sweeter than honey to kiss
And her slender angel's body
Felt so warm and tender in my arms
As in that brief moment in time
I held her closer and closer to me
So into her angel eyes I could look
And her sweet angel lips I could kiss
But that brief moment in time was my dreams
My very happy dreams of both night and day.

Donald John Tye

The Old City Walls Of Newcastle

In the dim and distant days to keep the town secure,
Newcastle was surrounded by a mighty strong stone wall,
surviving through the centuries, standing firm and tall.
Even at the present day, parts of it endure.

One of these is in a street known as Old Bath Lane,
where there is, at intervals a high imposing tower,
a look out post with slits to give our soldiers chance to scour
the landscape, meaning that no foe a stranglehold could gain.

All through the centuries these strongholds still remained,
but not in use because they were not needed anymore.
And so it was decided to renovate the floor
of one of them for meetings so its use was then regained.

I would often go there to a special get-together
in the nineteen forties at the ending of the war.
Northumbrian pipers played as we gaily took the floor
to trip around the room with the lightness of a feather.

Doing Scottish dances, Northumbrian ones too,
bowing to our partners, some of whom were wearing kilts,
we took up our positions, while we listened to the lilts
of the happy country music as we waited for our cue.

Back and forward, up and down, round and round we went,
reaching out our hands, clasping in an eightsome reel
or romping in a Morpeth rant, till unable to conceal
that we were out of breath and all our energy was spent.

Even now the walls still stand, and guides take visitors around
from Newcastle Civic Centre to review the different sites
where isolated walls remain to recall the many fights
in which they helped to vanquish foes while soldiers stood their ground

These walls have kept Newcastle safe and helped to make her great.
Geordies take enormous pride in their ancient Roman town
once called Novocastria, a place of world renown,
which Grainger and John Dobson endeavoured to create.

'Wherever ye gan ye're sure to meet a Geordie' so they say,
and Geordies are the finest folks on earth,
with their Geordie friendliness and Geordie mirth
and sense of humour both at work and play.

Kathleen McGowan

BEYOND THE SUMMER SUN

An old man sat in the park.
I watched his quiet fun
as he opened up his shirt
and enjoyed the sun.

Around him lovely flowers,
the weather has been fine.
Rows of poppies gleamed on the slopes,
like streams of red, red wine.

Some leaves fell into his hat,
which he refused to hold,
silent gifts from nearby trees
a few pieces of autumnal gold.

This caused him to contemplate
if it could be fair,
among the scents and hues of summer,
a hint of autumn in the air

He felt blessed by what he saw
in the beauty of the day,
yet from all this blazing stillness
the wandering birds flew away.

He sat there long with his thoughts,
until the light grew dim,
his figure blurred by evening mist,
like my memory of him.

Tony Gyimes

DREAMING

They say I'm a dreamer
And I suppose it's true.
I dream all day and night-time too
Of living life with you.
I dream of the beginning
When man and God were one
Oh Adam how He loved you
His first created son
Companion, friend you walked and talked
Unclothed but not ashamed
He gave you a helper
Eve is how she's named
A luscious fragrant garden
He didn't ask for much
Just tend it and be happy
But one tree you must not touch
The years of love and fellowship
In Eden were spent
Man and God together all things were content
God poured His love on both of you
You poured it back
And glorified the Creator that you knew
But on that dreadful day
When of that fruit you did bite
You broke your Father's precious heart
And He turned from your sight
And now the battle did begin
All because of Adam's sin
Oh fallen man how sad
The love that you'd been given
Now directed on yourself
Instead of God in Heaven.

Irene Rogerson

I Count

I stood perfectly still and held my breath, for I knew
Someone had made a very stupid mistake and I was stuck
And unable to get out of the Halifax in time.
Then of course I counted and waited for the bang.

I did check, honestly, and there it was in the stowage,
So it was perfectly safe to select the circuits of the bomb load,
As the photoflash of enormous power wasn't there . . .
But an anxious erk had replaced it.

So there I stood, having heard the photoflash slide out,
With a whoosh down the chute, but to where? And when?
Then my heart slowed down and still alive I fixed it,
And I am here to write about it all.

At least till the next time, which was soon, for a Halifax
Crashed on take-off; with a full load of bombs and fuel,
And I was the duty armourer of course,
So had to make sure that all was safe.

Quite simple on the face of it, till I got there and found
An empty aircraft from which the whole crew had gone,
And a cloud of 100 octane fuel all round,
And every bloody switch in the aircraft on.

It was easy to reach the 'accs', but hand on switch,
I recalled the occasional fat spark you got switching off,
And the swirling cloud of fuel in the air as well as
The two 1000lb bombs and the incendiaries.

There was no bravery, or even desperation; I did it
Because I was there to do exactly that, then on my bike
And off as fast the aircrew before me,
To count when I was a safe distance away

As I lay under the radio-active source I counted.
Nothing new about this, for I always have done under stress
But I didn't just count, for I snarled 'Die you bugger, die'
As I lay, hoping and praying for the thing to die inside me.

But it did not die, so I am still counting twenty years on,
When I change what passes for the bladder which failed me
And so was removed and thrown away, with other bits,
Which saved me, so I count to be sure that the new bit sticks on.

And I count the days since you died and left me
And the months and the empty, wasted years . . .
Oh God, what's the use of counting?

A S Walton

THE UKE

For 35 years, with just a little trying,
I have been able to hear the muffled strum
of this ukulele and hear his voice - Bing, Nat
and Jim Reeves through a membrane of Geordie.

It is a banjolele with a skin over the sound box
brown and worn by his fingers long ago,
fret grooves show his favourite three-chord bash.
He cradled it in his jumper.

'Where is the girl who was stolen from me
where is she, where is she now?
I miss her kisses wherever I go
how she haunts me, how she haunts me.
love plays a tune on the strings of my heart
just like a broken melody,
and wherever she has gone, she's the only one
God send her back to me.'

From the spools of that early tape recorder
it cuts through the times of my growing-up
and reaches me now.
The uke is in bits.
I could mend and restore it,
a project for winter nights.
Or just put it back together.
He's been 35 years dead.

Jack Bowden

WORTH'S THIEF

Do not judge by our outward vessels.
Rather judge by our inward souls.
For as with evil your holy soul wrestles,
So with trivial things your body scores goals.
Meaningless goals, like beauty and charm,
Which are but illusions and do sometimes harm.
For beauty and grace are judged alone.
People don't judge our innermost soul!
So, please, dear reader, look for the worth underneath,
And not judge the outer shell, which is worth's thief!

Christine M Wilkinson

PRIDE OF PLACE

There are times when we feel less than proud
of our county or borough or village;
perhaps we are under a cloud
of old stigma, say, murder or pillage.
We identify with where we're living,
feel our credit is somehow precarious
because some notorious misgiving
is part of our past; though vicarious,
the stigma feels very real to us:
we each take our share of the shame;
a masochist's yield to the tortuous
route that will exorcise blame.
It is fair that we suffer some measure
of discomfiture, as we do pleasure.

We are keen to accept all the praises
attaching by rights to our neighbours;
we glow as the bonfire blazes
on the strength of another man's labours.
Because we win Britain in Bloom,
enjoy the vast layout of flowers,
we feel that we planted that broom,
those carnations, as though they are ours.
Look when our Toon Army team scores,
and the scorer is borne shoulder-high,
we're up there to share the applause;
the emotion has caused us to cry.
We are part of the home we call base;
even passive, take pride in our place.

Adrian Brett

THE CHILDREN'S DREAM

It was twelve o'clock in the dead of night
Not a soul was to be seen in the pale moonlight
We flitted furtively from bush to tree
Deeper into Hylton Castle Woods where we wanted to be
The secret meeting place for my friends and me
Was a gnarled old stump, of a lightning struck oak tree.

Along the banks of the noisily bubbling stream,
Crossing a bridge lit by an autumnal moonbeam,
We saw the glade with its lush carpet of green,
The exact place our owners would see in their dreams
They would talk about it in the morning when they awoke,
In the kind of hushed tones in which children spoke

We listened intent to each word that they said
They talked non-stop since they'd risen from their bed,
But we had sat quiet and still as teddy bears do
We knew that what they'd seen was fact and quite true
For at that ball my girlfriend and I
Had danced in the woods 'neath the full moon in the sky,

Just before sunrise we left that fairy glade
It had been a huge success with our plans well laid
The ball we'd attended had been so grand
Fairy Tinkerbell had led us there by the hand
In the morning the children told their mother what they'd seen
But she told them, 'Don't be silly it's only a dream.'

R Marr

LOCAL COLLEGE

Most thinking men will thirst for more
Than just the social semaphore
Of sinking pints with dull chit-chats,
Exchanging hollow, cheap brick-bats.

In many pubs one often finds
Morosely drinking men whose minds
Disintegrate in talk that's drear
In stultifying atmosphere.

But on the Whitley Lodge Estate
You'll find the smart set integrate
In lofty and arcane discourse
Of academic intercourse.

There's talk of Socrates and Liszt,
Debate to analyse the gist
Of what comprises anti-matter,
And was Mozart a real mad-hatter?

The Kitti's men, its literati,
Parade as sparkling glitterati,
Expounding thoughts that one day might
Explain the constant speed of light.

To join this fellowship's debate
You might give pause and hesitate,
Bedazzled by the brainy patter
On topics that we all know matter.

But let me say you don't need knowledge
To join the Kitti's bar room college.
In fact the less you know of any topic
Equips you best to join the frolic!

Patrick Brady

MY SECRET MEMORIES

I've had a very mundane life
My wife and family have been my life
I've worked hard for them day by day
For very little take home pay

But there is something I want you to know
I've always had a secret drawer
No one knows what's there inside
Not that there's anything much to hide

Just some fantasy from the past
Of loves that were never meant to last
But it's lovely to look down memory lane
These days can't come back again

Now that I'm rapidly getting older
I'm gradually getting a little bolder
Why shouldn't I have my secret drawer?
I didn't really want anyone to know!

Sylvia McGregor

THE AIR SHOW

Aircraft flying, wings that glisten
Booming past, another mission
Loop the loop or level flight
Glad it's never held at night

Spectators gather, hear the roar
As up above the aircraft soar
Dive down fast, and then pull up quick
Amazes me how they're not sick

Displays galore as people throng
Wander round and catch the song
Radio stations playing loud
Noisy sounds just for the crowd

Yet year-by year they do return
Spend their money that they earn
Hot dog and a drink or two
Standing in that flaming queue!

Announcer booming, no one hears
Stand too close it hurts your ears
Suddenly a whoosh gone by
A hazy shape up in the sky

Helicopters tuck-tuck past
Wait all day; they're here at last
Spitfire and the Hurricane too
Remind us of the long lost few!

Parachutists drop from high
Flutter down as clouds roll by
Bang on target, a bull's eye!
Make it look a piece of pie

Children stare, their mouths agog
Concentrate like a silent log
Eyes so wide with wonder too
When they grow up, they want to do!

Dream of being a pilot now
Years go by then wonder how
A different job they settled for
Still right now they stare with awe!

Different yet the same to eyes
As year on year it multiplies
But we'll be back again God willing
Watch this space our air show's thrilling!

Neal Wright

THE ROOM

There is a room I love in the house of England
Sitting there, right up on the uppermost floor.
Almost forgotten by those down in the parlour.
No use at all to them, so close the door.

Uncaring, they never trouble to climb the winding stairs.
To see what hidden treasures they may find.
The room seems cold, the floorboards old and creaking
But the people in the parlour are very deaf and blind.

Through smoked up windows draped with long sand curtains
Lies a sea which welcomed ships to the stately home.
And from this sea came the gas, the oil, the coal
To make its owners rich, and keep them warm.

There is a repressed family living in that distant room
Their warmth defies the cold winds that beat down on the earth
They are the treasures of the household
They have added value to its worth.

The people in the parlour took life easy
Whilst the family built ships and trains upon their floor
Electricity was born to keep the household running
No use for the room now, close the door.

One day, who knows, the house may get new owners.
They'll climb the stairs and open up the door.
They'll welcome back the family to the household
And bring that distant room to life once more.

G D Wilson

WINTER WHEAT

Curl ice branch, heavy drift
across the snowfield
washcloud fast skies
faster rise
in perpetuum
gull arc and steeple

Kingly light
anointed in turbulent air
suckled on turbulent land
of root and choir
dusk and daughter tear
to flood fast.

Richard Leitch

The Tinker Girl

Suddenly she appeared.
Out of a close.
A tinker girl in ragged clothes
Who stopped and barred my way.
She raised her hands towards my face
I could not turn away.
But opened my handbag
Willing to give
To a small beggar child
Who needed to live
But quick as a flash
She snatched my purse
She meant to leave me
There in the lurch.
Before she escaped
I slapped those hands
Hands once were begging
Now turned to thieving.
So shyly at first
Now so deceiving
Taking my purse
'No, no' I said
'Nothing for you
A scolding instead'
She looked at me
With an evil eye
And cursed and left me
Standing by
She disappeared into the close
This tinker girl
In ragged clothes.

But far above
A curtain was twitched
By an unseen hand
The hand of a witch
A witch who was teaching
A small hand to thieve
This was the culprit I truly believe.

Maisie Bell

THE TOON ARMY

Grown men blubber, children cry, women mop their tears,
World disasters pale to nought, they've realised their fears.
There can't be worse scenarios, there can't be greater pain,
The agony of loss so great - it's happening again.

Not long to go, the stage is set, the world is looking on;
The rock on which their world revolves is shaky, almost gone.
Can they survive the absolute, the total devastation?
No, no! They've lost their purpose, all the meaning of creation.

Grief-stricken, heads in hands they sit dejected, all hopes past,
Just ninety minutes gone, spirits are low and eyes downcast.
Loud sobbing, wailing, weeping, howling, crying rends the air,
Thousands of grieving people wallowing in bleak despair.

Why? You may ask - what is the cause of this great British grief?
It's Shearer's penalty gone wide that beggars all belief.
Like me you may consider that the Geordies are all barmy,
But they're the intelligentsia of the North - the 'Great Toon Army'!

Gwen Stone

A Fraternal Settlement

Very few were we,
small-holdings on the isle,
wind-swept, our poverty
our way of life - denial.

My gentle brothers clad in brown
huddle in silent prayers together,
then later stoop to tasks unknown
to man or beast beyond the heather.

Close-knit community,
our souls silent gentle search,
through our pains and sincerity
for some small spark to enrich -

this barren wintry life
though enriched with love and faith,
but still denying, the continuous strife,
we gather resources for better days.

Silent stand our rock-like walls,
totally encrusted with glistening snails,
we pore over the book intent,
the tallow's light wavering with the vent -

where draughts whistle regularly
and we are often ill and sore,
but discipline exhorts finally,
there our souls learn to endure.

Heather Charnley

ROOM FOR IMPROVEMENT

Here is the would-be-fit at the gymnasium
Hoping to tone up her thighs and her lazy tum,
Carrying her trainers, carrying her 'cos'
And the special shampoo that comes from Oz.
Enters the changing room clutching her locker key -
Up until now she's been feeling quite frolicky!
All shapes and sizes of nude women vie
For a space in the towel-dance, trying to get dry.
Off with her street clothes and on with her gear -
Lycra's not kind when the bulges appear!
Pounding the treadmill, pedalling the bike,
She'd much rather be in fresh air on a hike
Or roasting a joint they'd eat later for dinner.
Is it really important that she should be thinner?
Reaches and twists like a flourishing vine -
Her age is against her, but she's doing fine.
Into the pool now, still thinking of food
And wondering how she appears in the nude
To the svelte and the saggy, the curved and the thin
Who are sisters only deep under the skin.
Twenty lengths crawled, now tries the jacuzzi,
Lies back and relaxes, begins to feel woozy
So off to the sauna to sweat off an ounce
And then a cold shower makes the goose pimples bounce.
Back in the changing room, queues for a warm shower,
And stands on the scales. In the previous hour
She has lost not a gram and her belly still wobbles
As though she is riding a bike over cobbles.
She ruefully laughs and her double chin shakes -
Thinks she'll go home and make chocolate tray bakes.
Uses the shampoo which promises locks
Which shine like the sun; hers look more like old socks.
Dresses to cover the bumps and the wrinkles
In clothes which the locker has pressed into crinkles.

Feels she's in desperate need of a coffee
(Perhaps with a flapjack or slice of banoffee).
Ponders, as cafewards she makes her move:
In which of these rooms is she meant to improve?

Christine Wylie

My County

Since the dawn of time my county has stretched,
From mountains across plains to the sea.
The Picts and Scots came from the north,
Then Romans from over the channel.
Roads and towns and forts they left,
Coins and books in Latin as well.
Vikings came out of the sea in hordes,
And built us our city of York.
Saxons came up from Wessex then,
And quickly showed them the door.
Normans told Wessex they were in charge,
Quickly ousting the Saxon king.

Each in their turn have left their mark,
Monuments and pillars abound.
But most of all they left something to us,
That most are forgetting to use.
We are Yorkshire tykes and well bred,
But not when you hear us talk.
Dialect is a language special to us,
You've to listen to every word.
A warning I must give you first,
Depending the district you stay.
Each one had its own dialect tongue,
And to count them there are ninety-three.

We've ports where the fishermen bring in their catch,
Scarborough, Whitby and Staithes.
Freighters they come to Kingston-on-Hull,
That's on the great Humber river.
Factories on the rivers and farms on the plains,
With beauty spots all round the Dales.

So when you come and visit us here,
Be sure to fetch plenty of brass!
We've cities and towns and villages too,
With scenery the best in the land.
We'll show you our wares, the best you can get,
Sell you plenty of gifts to take back.

Kenneth Copley

THERE'S NOWT ASTRUE AS YORKSHIRE FOLK

I wonder what people think of Yorkshire?
What images spring to mind,
Do they really think it's the land of miners?
When the pits been shut for a time.
All they eat is Yorkshire pudding,
Na, that's really not true!
We eat other stuff, fish and chips, tripe and curry.
You think we all wear flat caps, yer some do,
Their dogs are all whippets, I think not!
They say we don't half talk funny,
But that's the Yorkshire slang for you.
We folk are a helpful and friendly lot,
All the brass we've got tha knows we'd give,
You, every blooming lot . . . tha thinks not.
Thas nowt as queer as Yorkshire folk,
There's nowt as true.

Leeanne Shires

ENDEAVOUR 2002

A steady drip of crystal gleam
On mossy stones in darkened dell
Outside the wind wails loud and clean
Sweeping all before, pell-mell

Did Cathy range this moorland, wild,
Bereft of home and hearth and soul?
Where rugged folk down valleys mild
Gaze up at sheep and rock and knoll

But that was many ages past
Those folk have long since left the land
Except, hold still, I hear 'Avast!'
A whispered word, a shanty band

Above the Abbey's sun-set stone
A stately ship with sails like wings,
Ploughs through the brine and harbour's foam
Endeavour's mast and rigging sings

The melody is old and proud
This is no ghost of history past
For this is Yorkshire - loud and bold
The motif of our land so vast

Anne Aitchison

Untitled

Do you ever wonder
As you go rushing by?
Or do you even notice
A person such as I?
The wheelchair is my prison
Don't I have a point of view?
My brain is very active
I wish my legs were too.
Do you have to ask my partner
What I'd like to eat or drink?
I still have an opinion
And the capacity to think.
Next time that you meet someone
Not quite as fit as you
Please give a word of welcome
It could be you or you or you.

Mollie Sanderson

EIGHTEENTH CENTURY LOVERS

Oh lordly lover art thou sleeping?
Awake, for dawn comes softly creeping.
The glistering stars dim, one by one
And birds begin their morning song.

Oh Lordly lover haste thee now
The farmer's cock begins to crow,
Thy horse is pawing at the ground
Perchance someone should hear the sound.

Oh Lordly lover time is fleeting
Hear my heart so quickly beating,
I dare not hurt my father's pride,
His daughter dear, a shotgun bride.

Oh Lordly love, your riding crop
Now through the casement gently drop,
Psst! My dear, your glove, your glove
Goodnight, God speed, my Lordly love.

Pauline M Parlour

UNTITLED

People stop, people stare
At handicapped children, they don't care
They laugh at them and call them names
But underneath, we're all the same

Those who are deaf, those that are dumb
Those that cannot see
Those who are lame, that cannot walk
They're still the same as me.

Autistic children, in a world of their own
They just want to be alone
They're so full of love
That cannot be shown

It breaks my heart to know
Why people are so cruel
Everybody's loved and made by God
And that's the golden rule.

M Simpson

THANK YOU
(Dedicated to my mum, Glynis.
I love you)

Thank you, you made my life worth living
Wiping my tears and the love you were giving
Thanks to your loving, it got me through
I wouldn't be here now, if it wasn't for you!
You've been by my side, day after day
You were the love that never faded away
Thank you for not leaving, you never let go
I know that through life, you'll be my hero.
You make me feel proud to know you're mine
My own flesh and blood right down the line
You gave me my dreams and made them come true
There's one person to thank . . . that's you!
My hand reaches for you, you lead the way
Down each path and through each day
I've never known a love to be so strong
With a mother like you it will always carry on
You've been my friend and looked on as my dad
Through each and every happy time and also the bad
Each time I was in pain, each time that I cried
With your loving arms and words, the tears dried.
You to me are so special, the love I could never describe
No other person could replace the love I have inside
The heart I have stays healthy, the feelings I have are true
I thank God for making a person . . . A lady so special as you!

Janine Williams

IN THE LION'S DEN

I always know where you'll be;
So I sit there long enough,
And you come to me
And in that moment.
I'm in the limelight of your eyes;
I'm in Nirvana:
I've won every prize
Then you dart away;
And I'm left to watch,
As you work the room.
Like the moon works the clocks.
And in that moment,
It all becomes clear;
Trying to hold you down,
Is like trying to catch the wind
With a spear.

Rachel C Zaino

WORD PAINTING

I wish that I could paint for you,
A green and foam-flecked sea.
Or a luminescent moon of palest ivory.

I would create a sylvan scene,
With bluebell wood and winding stream,
Where golden fishes dart and gleam.

With brush on canvas I'd depict,
White clouds on an azure sky,
And the delicate tracery
On the wings of a dragonfly.

I would imbue with colour bright,
The yellow glow of candlelight
And softly shining stars of night.

I wish I could portray a view,
Of an evening sunset's rosy hue,
Or the silver mist of morning dew.

But I am not an artist
With fingers deft - it's true!
And so I paint these scenes in words,
To present my dear to you!

N V Wright

DERBY DAY

He was lost, my little brother,
At the races;
Only four or so he was,
The sky clear blue,
A heat haze,
Perfect picnic weather;
Loose change,
Just a bob or two,
In Dad's coat pocket
After bus fares;
Not that he'd let on to Mum
What he would do with it.
We only went to taste the atmosphere,
Saw nothing of the racecourse.
Mum - she disapproved -
Of racing? . . . betting?
We weren't sure;
She disapproved a lot
In those days.
So we sat, excitement roaring through the air,
With white jam sandwiches
And orange juice.
Dad sauntered off
'To see what's what,'
A snatch of freedom
With his ready money.

Then he disappeared,
My brother,
There one minute
Gone the next.
We looked for him in widening circles,
Taking in the near perimeter of racetrack,
Milling crowds and frantic bookies,
None more frantic than my mum.

An hour or so we searched
In vain, until, across the field
We saw him, hand in hand and chatting
With the policeman,
None the worse.
My mum was mortified,
The rest of us relieved.
Just then, oblivious, Dad came dawdling back
In time to get the blame.

Dee Yates

MY CHILDREN'S EYES

Don't cry for me when I am gone
My life must end but my soul lives on
My soul is for ever and never dies
It lives eternal in my children's eyes

The time will come when I must go
But my spirit will stay and this I know
Death is the spector that I despise
But my soul is still there in my children's eyes

Don't mourn for me. Look back and smile
The tears and pain only stay for a while
Just think of me but please don't cry
I will always be there in my children's eyes

The years go on and the seasons too
But what stays and grows is my love for you
My soul lives on, my love grows in size
They are those beautiful sparkles in my children's eyes

Remember the happy times about my life
For the sorrow of death can cut like a knife
I'll always be with you from the moment you rise
I'm with you forever in my children's eyes

Gareth Thorpe

GARDEN

You are like a clear green stone
I want to fold up and put in my pocket.
In you the tedious rules of space are reversed -
I have stumbled on a universe,
Ruled by a fence and a ring of earth.
Thick crystalline light pours from the trees
Slows the hands on the church tower,
Your silent beauty comforts as a mother's love
Making the air sparkle for joy.
Even the great oaks are dancing
Smoothing heavy heads in the river of smiling ghosts.

Sitting studying, I breathe in memories
To be stored in the crevices of my lungs -
So now I can see him, again and again,
Walking in the garden in the cool of the day,
A restored Adam.

Ailsa McDermid

DEPRESSION

Depression the doctor would say
take these pills and go away
he did not see beyond the mask
the clouds of thunder gathering fast.

The pressure building and building,
until my head would spin,
Help me someone, take me under your wing.

No one sees beyond the mask
the turmoil within growing fast,
How long will this last, this unseen pain,
will the mask fall a little, will she show her pain.

Do those close to her, see her despair
or are they too busy
or don't they bloody-well care!

Anne Dunkerley

THE FRIDAY FOOTERS

The third Friday of each month we all gather,
An elite band of just seven or eight,
Leaving Leeds City behind
Because we are all so inclined,
And woe betide anyone who comes late.

Mavis and Ian, they are my close family,
Sister and brother-in-law, also from Leeds,
David - the distance walker,
Muriel - the great talker,
Ted and Shirley - both fit as fleas.

Then there's my better half, my dear Colin,
My strength, for all to see,
Without him I'd be lost,
It would come at great cost,
And to complete the happy band - there's me.

We don on our boots and our rucksacks,
Walking sticks, all to the fore,
Forget potions and pills,
And head for the hills,
Clambering over stiles and the moor.

Yorkshire is a wonderful county,
The hills and the dales are the best,
With time to spare,
We enjoy the peace and fresh air.
So good for the soul and the chest!

Sylvia A Whitaker

The Rhythm Of Love

Capture me a floating seed
fresh from the dandelion clock
encage it tightly within your hand
listen to its sleepy tick-tock.

Tell me the time, the season, the year
for then I'll give you my heart
and though the winds of time will pass
I promise we'll never part.

Pick me a bluebell from the meadow over yonder
the bluest and prettiest of all
and if you come back with the finest my love
under your spell I will fall.

Bring me some honey, so pure, so sweet
straight from the hive so new
so I might taste it and think I'm in Heaven
and standing beside me is you.

Catherine Watson

CONFINED

If my body was as active as my imagination,
Think of the things I could do, if there were no limitations.
If I could just get up and walk out of the door
I could watch the sunlight flitting over the moor.
Glimpse bobtails disappearing into a bolt
Enjoy the crazy ballet of a newly born colt.
I could climb a mountain and touch the sky,
Swim in the ocean, run through the rye.
Cultivate the earth and make things grow.
Leave footprints in the sand or virgin snow.
Take my children on a picnic amongst the bluebells
Or down to the beach in search of seashells.
I can only sit here and imagine what if
My bones were stronger and my muscles less stiff.
Being pushed around in this wheelchair is such a bind,
But please Lord; don't take away the power of my mind.

Megan Ward

THE RIVER CALDER

Gently through Brighouse town
The River Calder wends its way,
Born on the Pennine moorlands
It flows on day by day.

Its banks do twist and turn
Through countryside so fair,
Until at last at Castleford
It joins the River Aire.

I have watched the gentle Calder
Through the seasons of the year,
In winter raging waters
Cover every river weir.

In summer months above the spume
Look for the kingfisher in flight,
Whilst damsel and dragonflies
Present a glorious sight.

Four thousand years ago
The River Calder was first born
And it will still be rolling
When I am long, long gone.

David A Garside

SLEEPLESS

My mind is in a turmoil,
I cannot get to sleep.
The day's events come crowding in;
Into my thoughts they creep;
Rushing round until
The thoughts spill
Out in a jumble:
The ideas tumble
Like cartwheels,
Head over heels

I turn my head on my pillow;
I toss from side to side;
I lie there sleepless in the night,
No matter how I've tried.
To me, sleep is denied;
An overactive brain . . .
Oh! Just to sleep again!

Rosalind I Caygill

UNTITLED

Last night I took a walk around
The town where I was born
Past the church of Saint Mary's
With its flags all ragged and torn.
I walked down past the factories
Belching smoke into the sky
And through the haze my memories
Still bring tears to my eyes.

Down past the old iron foundry
And the disused flour mill
Where my time on Earth was moulded
And part of me is still.
Along past terraced houses
Where we'd steal sweets from the shops
And though we never had too much
We were happy with what we'd got.

Onwards through the dusty roads
And the overgrown playing fields
By the market and the hospital
Where old wounds never heal.
The march of time is endless
As it tramples on the past
And I'm surrounded now by concrete
As I search a blade of grass.

In far flung years I had the power
I was master of all I surveyed
But with the eyes of experience
I see no beauty in decay.
I walk down past the schoolyard
Where the children scream and shout
They have no love for this town
Just their dreams of getting out.

If only I could stay a while
And watch the children play
Let their laughter fill my senses
As I dream of yesterday.
Now my dreams have turned to nightmares
My time is all but spent
In the streets of recollection
Of where my childhood went.

John Gill

Poppy The Heroine

This is the story of Poppy Green
And how she became a heroine.
As a child she was her parents' little princess.
But as she grew through her teens, her life was a mess.

For pride and ambition she cared not a jot
And everything started going to pot.
She followed a path that none could predict
When she became a drug addict.

She thought she would try her friends to impress
By smoking a joint of cannabis.
In her knowledge she had now filled a gap
And found that she needed a spliff or a wrap.

After months of smoking the weed
She did not feel quite up to speed
So she took a small pill on a clubbing spree
And spent the night in ecstasy.

When she woke in the morning her condition was plain
So she took a sniff of crack cocaine
The people she mixed with urged her to sin
And she started injecting heroin.

She shared her needles with smackheads
And lay down comatosed on filthy beds.
As the blood in her body spread the drug to her brain
Her senses rose to a higher plane.

When the effects wore off and the drug was no more
She discovered now that she knew the score
The priority which in her mind did nag
Was to get on the streets to obtain the scag.

It was a struggle soon to get the gear
When her cravings became severe.
Sometimes her body felt so bereft
She even had to resort to theft.

To get the money to fund the habit
She'd rob a house or smash and grab it.
With cash in hand she would do a deal
And obtain a fix to make life unreal.

She ignored the facts so plain to see
That some of her friends contracted Hep B.
As to drug purity the dealer lied
Poppy O.D'd and nearly died.

She was snatched back from the brink of death;
Some sense in her brain said this could be your last breath.
She suddenly developed a will to live
To beat this addiction every effort she'd give.

To save her life it was quite plain
She would have to stop shooting up in vein.
A detox battle would have to be fought
Her friends and relations gave their support.

She started a programme of Methadone
With counsellors' help, she was not alone.
After long months of struggle now she is clean
And Poppy has become a heroine.

Patsy Preshaw

WILLIAM'S BOOTS

He left his boots behind.
Why should that
bring tears to my eyes?
His Easter excesses -
too many eggs -
had erupted violently,
over his coat,
over my carpet
and over his boots.

Why tears?
The boots will need cleaning
before posting them back,
evidence showing in lace and tongue
of young William's over indulgence.
No problem.

So why tears?
The boots look so small and so vulnerable -
just like him.
What will he make of the world,
this three year old with the probing mind?
Will he step steadily forward,
tho' marching to the tune of a different drum?
Or will the boot have a sadder, more sombre significance?
Hence the tears.

Daphne Clarke

PORTRAIT IN SEPIA

Herring girls cutting and slicing with their razor sharp knives
the steel-blue fishes dragged from the sulky sea.

That was in the long ago of this town, caught up in a dross
of knick-knacks, kiss-me-quicks, ice cream cornucopias
and spun-glass candyfloss.

No one now sits gazing at the sailor-blue sea,
noise, spumes up in spirals of sand,
salt-moated castles fly shuddering pennants
of uncertain lands, doomed to the serpent gliding sea.

Elizabeth Rimington

THE AFTERMATH OF SEPARATION

I keep wondering how it came to this,
Those goodbye tears and farewell kiss.
How my life reached this nadir
From a state of nirvana bliss.

I still smell the fragrance of her perfume
Lingering on in what was once our room.
An aroma of wilted flowers
From this now faded bloom.

At night, my dreams still speak her name,
A subconscious spark to ignite my pain.
Memories sifting through the ash
Of our now extinguished flame.

Recollections of her parting words
Those 'I'll always love you' now seem absurd.
Just platitudes of separation
I wish I had never heard.

So I keep wondering and swallowing,
This self pity I keep wallowing in.
Knowing that it will choke all hope
For any further love following.

Keith Tissington

THE REUNION
(ODE TO AIREBORO GRAMMAR 1988)

Tonight we are gathered, school chums of
yesteryear, to chat and laugh with each other over
wine, or a glass of beer. To recall happy memories,
maybe some sad. But we'll reminisce and cogitate
over the times we had - those mock air raids,
running helter-skelter, clothes half on or off
(from doing gym) dashing to the shelter.
The swimming pool, shallow dives! We couldn't go
deep. Excuses - 'Please Miss, varrucas on mi feet.'
Biology - pumping lungs, dissecting rabbits and
frogs. Windows thrown wide and 'exercise', if we sat
'like logs'! Gym and games, good for our figures;
art class and 'That nude man', brought on our
sniggers! School choir, school trips - mostly Bolton Abbey.
Being proud of our school - not daring to
appear shabby! Thinking of all our teachers,
a dedicated crowd, suffice to say folks - they really
'did us proud'. There was no 'shilly shally',
no let up or complaint. Maybe a little sexist, only
boys got the cane! So three cheers for Aireboro Grammar,
hip, hip, hooray. Attending there in the 40's
has made us what we are today.

Barbara Buckley

WHAT HE DID YESTERDAY

What he did yesterday? Why, what does it matter?
Yesterday is gone! Now, is the present.
Where we plan for tomorrow.
We look forward to the new day approaching
But only the back is turned on yesterday.

Thoughts on yesterday are but memories,
Try as you will
The repeat performance will never be the same.
They rest in the mind, awaiting as it were
Their own burial.

'Tis as if, loving a dream, 'tis gone!
Something new, revolutionary, resplendent
Replaces that dream!
Down to earth common sense, and reality
Step forth, hand in hand.

Ready to meet and hail tomorrow's theme
Whatever it may be!
Sentiments of yesterday wane
As does an old garment,
Then on with new uniform, come soldier on!

Life is not here to stand at ease
Watching the sun rise and set
For that performance is routine and recurs.
Seek for the light of a new horizon,
Its rays glistening on the new, the young.

Which day by day are cherished
Rooting, springing, growing, budding
Till in its fullness, the flower blooms.
When the bloom has withered and gone
What is it but yesterday's memory?

Cherishing still,
The newness, the growing, the peak.
Does fate plan the scenes of today and tomorrow
That yesterday might receive
And hold those dreams?

Mary Dearnley

YORKSHIRE

Heatherclad moors and the sea and the dales
This is the county I love.
When God made Yorkshire He must have been
Smiling with joy from above!

I often go on trips around the world
I travel by 'plane and sea.
I gaze at so many wonderful things
But Yorkshire's the place for me!

When I'm coming home I'm so glad to be
Back in the biggest and best.
The rolling green fells and the drystone walls
That's where I'll be laid to rest!

Home is where the heart is - that's what they say
And I do believe it's true.
But my home must always be in Yorkshire
So my heart will stay there too!

Nancy Walecka

REFLECTION

The sun is out, a wonderful day,
Through all the grey patches in my life I see only the light,
The buds are appearing, if they can weather the storm, then so can I.
A very inspiring time for me, the start of spring,
As the buds break through, a surge of energy makes me start to
                                                                         bud inside

Through the rest of the year I strive to blossom,
Perhaps this year I will flower to my full potential.
May I receive the energy and light I need to bloom,
In glorious colour and strength, strong roots and stem, with soft
                                                            colourful aromatic petals,
The kind that people will love to touch and share in its beauty.

Sue Lupton

A Face From The Past

Near by me stands an elderly lady
Soberly dressed in an elderly way
We stood in the queue, side by side
Did she know me? She didn't say
I hadn't seen her for many a year
I thought that I knew her face
It was only when I heard her voice
I remembered, another time and place
When we were young
We knew each other
From dances - boys - and things
When we were young and beautiful
My God, what ageing brings
We paid our bills together
Then we both went on our way
If she knew me as I knew her
She left and didn't say

Molly Ann Kean

HOLIDAY TIME

Swimming in the sea, relaxing in the sun
Work is over, holiday has begun
Waves are lapping on the shore
Pina colada, yes I'll have one more

Lunch of fresh fish, only just caught
Trips to the markets, souvenirs bought
Barbecues at sunset and warm balmy nights
Trips on boats, see all the sights

Photographs taken for when I get back
Holiday over, must go and pack!

A Thornton

WHEELDALE

Betimes I seek the lonely glade,
The paths trod more by sheep than man,
Where none profane should dare intrude,
Or prying eyes its secrets scan,
Where I may learn as from wise book
The lore that speaks in the swift brook.

The rocks that like some ruined site
Surmount the hillock - reedy sedge -
Birch-grove that shields from breeze and sight -
Kind shelter of o'erhanging edge -
Oh! In such sacred spots as these
I know the woodland deities!

Not as the high Hippolytus
Fit consort for the forest queen,
Though I should live anonymous
Still I, her courtier have been,
And find my ample recompense
In sweet enchantment of the sense.

Barrie Williams

ALL MIXED UP

You came to me like a little child
Your love you offered with all your might
I held your hand, you squeezed it tight
I wasn't ready for you that night

Although I loved you and you wanted me
We were all mixed up, you and me
A broken marriage we had both left behind
Just your loving friend, I wanted to be

You then went berserk, you played about
Wild oats you had to sow
First one Madam Butterfly, then another and another
No fulfilment could you find

You found no one to love and care for
A broken man, you appear to me when you say
With me you want to start again
My reaction, which has to be will be

Hetty Foster

Icara, This Winter
(Lepa Sela Lepo Gore) *

Given half a chance
I'd be flying south
this winter, Icara sighed

Bloodshot eyes contracting
on the tail-back lights
red-dotting a motorway curve
beyond Brighouse

And it's downhill, all the way
You used to tease, foot
hard on the accelerator

Thirty years ago
the pack of pills in my pocket
spelt a bare-back ride

and not half! By now
we were past a count
of awkward single beds
we'd managed to share

with belly to tear-jerking guffaws.
I, you insisted, right up to the
bitterest lemon of ends

was a definite Ratty
to your ongoing Moley
as the wind whispered
countless invitations

through our willow past
midnight. Children of the mid-war
stringencies we warmed from the first
glance to each other's version

of the past: shared thoughts on Civil War
necessities, sadly, sometimes;
sang The Internationale, you taught me

in a hotchpotch of languages. We laughed;
the tune remained the same, underlying
a bond beyond any closed door domesticity

Trees we got planted down Scarletts Road
may have outlasted our attempts
to keep all the balls soaring

and, batten down the hatches, all ship-shape
Bristol fashion! against a magnificent folie
à deux; increasingly exhausted, we had to
admit our love could fail
us.

Yet afterwards, after the final punctuation
of our mutual skin across the Kingdom of Fife
rural Essex and a kaleidoscope of Paris quarters;
impromptu escapes via the route to the relentless southern sun

you'd send me copy of your Auden, our Rosa Luxemburg
Austen's and Byron's letters; a little blue card
to raise funds for the '84 Miners' Strike.

Since I rode north, that arid March
another sun-dissolving day
a van jam-packed with my, some of your and some of our
shared things, I have no car

but memories waxing at odd times north and south
melting into rear lights without distinction.
And the untreated upper vertebrae

Whiplashed once during a stupid fratch
are notched, as though gnawed over time
by our home-grown dogs, obsessive as usual about
perfecting their little bones.

But hush, old love
the film has begun
'Lepa Sela, Lepo Gore' - *
one of the languages we might have invented
to amuse ourselves through Scottish nights
that once began in the afternoon at something to three

I am seeing as almost with you
side by side, thighs tight packed
out of blackness, a former country:

another desired success
which could still set the Continent alight

'Lepa Sela, Lepo Gore'
                        when love fails

* Serbo-Croat: Pretty Village, Pretty Flame (Director, Dragojevic 1996)

Anna Taylor

CORNUCOPIA CORNER

King cobra cowled beacon standard
snake charmed into suicidal list
dominates Portland screed, smiles
saving grace on barren base, lends
laconic, lengthwise light less
leeringly luminous leastways

then dawn's advancing illicit
glancing pry, ultimately stripping
naked faulty Indian ropetrick,
India rubber envelopes rolled in tread
to where internal juices bled their last

body shells from Hell that once
were Nirvana, Heaven sent, or
unattainable pinnacle of man's desire,
obsolescence, obscenity bound at conception

rosebay, convolvulus and chain
link fence lovingly caress where
Arthur takes delivery. Today it's

England plays Nigeria, half past
seven kick off, only river moves today

only river gives reflective slant.

Phillip Beverley

THE OTHER ME

As a boy I would stare with pride
At the other me, towering by my side
Turning my life into a dream of mine
With love to build and friendship to climb

I was his shadow, with him everywhere
My childhood friend and always there,
If I had to ask or wanted to know
The other me would tell me so

As I copy him, my roots grow
Then the other me becomes my shadow
Who's the other me? Not a king, god or cad
It's just pure and simple 'Dad'

With no friendly rivalry or enemies' deceit
Just the purest love for me
Just the purest love for me

Mark Wood

SORROW IN THE GARDEN

Bluebells lurking beneath the tree
Heads hung low, almost a bow
Are you sad, are you blue
Why do you hide beneath the plume
Masking your beauty from prying eyes?

Roses of red, in the passion of full bloom
Velvety soft, sweet smelling hue
Why do you weep, why do you cry?
Your dewdrops have fallen on stony ground
The thorns that guard you, are no use now
You're dying of sorrow, roses of red

Sweet William, in Technicolor array
Standing erect, guarding the way,
Why are you sad, with your nature so sweet?
Have you seen something, that's maybe not right
Perhaps the sun has failed to appear?

Lavender carpet, out of control
Catching each leg wandering along
Perfume so mellow which sends some asleep
Masked in fumes, of exotic perfume

Why are you all so sorrowful today?
The garden is rosy, and tranquillity reigns
Maybe not, said the tall climbing lilac
Songbird has fallen from out of my branches
No longer the sound of his cords shall we hear
Just the sound of silence
In the whispering air

Liz Macauley

FREEDOM OF THOUGHT

People in a far off land are dying
Their bereaved families are crying
And yet no one seems to care
After all they are not there
So why should all be concerned?
By now they should have learned
People fighting their neighbour
Slavers looking for cheap labour
Politicians argue and lie
Whilst the angels here cry
They cry for each of your sins
As they watch you do those things
Do you realise what goes on
In people's hearts that you stamp on?
Does it matter in the big picture
Do any of us really have a future?
What's to stop me from being dead?
And never seeing my son's head
Watch as the woman I love
Brings him into the world from above
What would I tell him about life?
About all of those people's strife
About the cost of living in England
About the man who's in command
About you and all of the rich
About that button, the switch
The things that can destroy
All of his friends and his favourite toy
Who gives you the right
To take my life in the night?

I am a free man in another land
And I want to hold his tiny hand
If you high class people kill more
There will be no one to open your door
Fighting is a last resort in my eye
My son has a right to live and die

Matthew Ayre

THE STEELMAKERS

In Sheffield there's a shopping mall
Well known to many, Meadowhall,
Free parking spaces surround outside,
And shoppers come from far and wide.
A Supertram runs from the city centre,
There's easy access where shoppers enter,
The streets have every kind of shop,
Where they can 'shop until they drop'.
When they're tired with aching feet
They can find a nearby seat,
Or places where they can get refreshment
In handy cafes or in a restaurant.

This place is built on the former site
Of a workplace of industrial might,
A place where chimneys emitted sulphurous smoke,
The atmosphere nearly made you choke,
Even the sparrows they said, had a cough,
To live nearby was really tough.
Those chimneys belching smoke and grime
Are just memories of the time
When this city's fame and reputation
Was known far and wide to every nation.
Huntsman and Bessemer led the way
To the steelmaking processes of today,
But where men toiled in the furnace heat
Now shoppers walk in a busy street.

But will this city's fame for steel and cutlery last
We know its fame stretches into the past,
For all who have read Chaucer knows,
'The miller wore a Sheffield dagger in his hose',
And though Chaucer wrote that six hundred years ago
All the history of cutlery we will never know,

But in that mall, as we pass by
Three bronze figures catch our eye,
There are places on them that brightly shine
Polished by others touch as well as mine,
And seeing those figures, we can but feel
Though cast in bronze they are 'men of steel',
So when you pass by them and you touch
Whisper 'Thanks, this city owes you much.'

Roy Dickinson

THE FOUR YORKSHIRE REGIONS

There were four young men from Yorkshire,
Who met twice a week in a pub,
One from every region, I believe,
North, south, east and west,
My tale not yet done.

One day they argued which one was the best,
So they thought up a test,
To tell each other
A little about each one;

The southerner mentioned Sheffield Steel,
And may I add, where my mother was born.

The man from the east, mentioned the Humber Bridge,
The biggest around
And to add, where the Trotters once came and made a film.

The man from the north, spoke about the beauty of the Dales,
And the surrounding coastline and Harrogate, the famous spa town.
And to add, James Herriot the author, where his writings were inspired.

The westerner who was listening very quietly,
Smiled and spoke wisely,
'This ale we drink now is brewed in the west, I believe,
Why do we all meet here,
Regular twice a week,
Drinking this beer?'

And so they all agreed,
That the west
Was the best,
And vowed never to argue the quest.

But each one knew
In their heart of hearts,
That they were all
Just as good as the rest.

Jane Milthorp

Dawn Chorus

In my bed
In the early morning
I listen to the dawn
Gently breaking.
I listen to the birds
To their sweet singing

And beyond, and beyond, and beyond . . .

I hear cars on the road,
Purring and humming
A mile away.
In the sky
A plane flying somewhere
Over the sea
And far away.

Deeper than that,
Beneath the surface
The sounds reach my ears
Of cows in the fields
Rhythmically munching
And treading their hooves
Into the paths they make
To travel in line, every day.

Down in the earth the badger curls
Closing his eyes
After his night's wanderings,
Folding himself into peaceful sleep,
Snuffling his mate as their noses meet.

Above the ground I hear buds uncurling
And petals unfurling to the morning sun.
I hear the stretch of the trees
As they lift up their branches
And the song of the wind
In the tender leaves.

The song of the wood
Crescendos around me
As I listen to spring
Waking up the world.
Her breath, her touch,
Her playful stirring
Make me feel
That life is good.

And beyond, and beyond and beyond . . .

I hear the stars go out
One by one
Closing their eyes
To the rising sun,
Sighing as quietly
They take their repose.
The moon glides silent
Behind the low hills,
Surrendering to
The arms of the wold.

In the town far away
I hear the clocks ticking
And the running of water
As bodies are washed
And dreams fade away
And the business of daytime
Regains its sway.
Children eat breakfast
And parents curse
Over homework, packed lunches
Trip money,
Giving chapter and verse
On doing one's best and not wasting time
That precious commodity
That goes before you realise . . .

And back in my bed
My thoughts turn away
From the hurly burly of another day,
They turn themselves inwards,
They listen quite hard
To the regular beating
Of my own small heart.

Jo Leak

KEEP TRYING

If we cannot be successful
The least that we can do is try,
Or we'll be labelled failures,
You don't want that, nor do I.

We all have our limitations,
Which if we try, we can surpass.
But if we surrender to them
We'll be letting down our class.

We must have aspirations
To reach our personal goal
And we must strive to reach it
Both with our heart and soul.

If you fail to reach your target
Having given all you've got
Cheer up! You're not a failure
For at least you had a shot.

Gordon Barnett

A TYKE'S TONGUE

'Dus tha know what I mean?'
Words of a Tyke never seen.
True Yorkshire tongue so grand,
Frequently spoken in Tyke land.
'See yeah!' Given in depart.
Fond farewell from the heart.
'Give over!' The end of jokes told,
Not a challenge to be bold.
'Soft bugger,' a wimp in weep,
Or a cover of sadness so deep.
'Shur up!' Stopping the argument state,
Not a brazen way to make it irate.
'Get owt of it!' Life's hard and long.
Understanding times will make you strong.
'Scared of nowt!' Words of strength,
Achieving all at any length.
'What's tha say?' Confused with the view,
Gaining time to think it all through.
'Young uns,' given to children so dear.
Losing it by growing, year by year.
'Are lass,' the only affection in life,
Girlfriend, fiancée or the wife.
So this is the Yorkshire tongue you hear,
Sometimes mis-read because it's not clear.
But to the Tyke, it is honest and clean,
'Dus tha now know what I mean?'

Gerald Elliott

WHITE PLUMES IN THE SUN

The check-out girl looks bored to tears as you fumble with your cash
Picks at a painted fingernail - she likes to cut a dash

To her you're just a tired old man, with stained and dirty tie
A nuisance to her check-out queue, and people passing by

But I remember, I remember, when I was very small
How you came on leave, a soldier, strong and young and tall

I remember, I remember hearing of all you'd done
But mostly I remember the white plumes in the sun

A-top a smart white uniform, with badge and buttons bold
The local lads were jealous, your image left them cold

They'd not compete for maidens fair with a newly fledged Marine
I reckon they were pleased as Punch, the day you left the scene

It's sad to see you lonely now, with all your battles won
It's hard to reconcile you with the white plumes in the sun

Outside there's an old man with swollen shuffling feet
Inside still tracks Ki-Kuyu through the steaming jungle heat

I fear age has no dignity, and there'll be worse to come
Unless it all ends quickly, as it mercifully does for some

But I'll remember, I'll remember, though your life is nearly done
A soldier smart, in uniform, and white plumes in the sun.

J Barker

A Poem About Fruit

Six lovely fruits you can eat for dessert
Oranges are juicy with vitamins too
Apples are good for your teeth and gums
Peaches are the finest fruit with cream
Or maybe you would like peaches with ice cream.

Grapes are in bunches, green and black
They grow on the grapevine and are made into wine.
Pears are a little funny in shape
Don't be put off when you taste it,
You will eat the lot.
Strawberries are the top fruit of all
Strawberry jam and crumble pie
Eat any fruit, it's good for your health,
It will help you through the day
And give you some strength.

Barbara Ann Hartley

FORCE OF THE SEA

I watched it flow,
Soft and graceful like a soaring bird.
I heard it singing,
Humming to the Gods above.
I felt the crash of it as it washed over me.
It became a part of me,
Close to me, touching me,
Covering me with its fresh array of colour,
The rainbow seemed to live within it.
Breathing its air,
Making my skin tingle.
I could touch it and not feel pain,
I could watch it forever,
Just flowing,
Always moving.
I may follow it someday,
To a better place,
To a holy place,
As this is my Heaven on Earth.

Rachel Harrison

Sunset To Sunrise

The sky is bright - it's late afternoon and the sun is sinking fast,
Colours blaze as clouds of gold, beyond the sky go past,
Pinks and yellows, golden flecked, what a heavenly sight,
Rainbow shades, turning bright as day turns into night.

Orange and grey and purple, flashes of red and blue,
Skies at the end of a lovely day, shine for me and you,
The sun is seeking its lowly bed, awaits another morn
To shine forth before your wondering eyes, and greet another dawn.

Tomorrow comes, lo and behold - another golden sky
Beyond belief, the colours spread, filling the watcher's eye,
And once again the day we greet, see many a coloured hue,
Seeing the gift of another dawn is there for us anew.

Birds arise and glide their way, like prayers upon the wing,
The church extols the happy hymns, the ones we love to sing.
So thank the Lord for feelings, the brilliance of his land
Awesome the colours that we've come to love, given by His hand.

Margaret M Warkup

BRIDLINGTON BEACH

Be it Bondi, the Costas, or Bridlington beach,
all have their particular appeal.
What draws us down to the water's edge,
standing on sand, or rocky ledge?

The infant with the bucket and spade,
elderly couples strolling the prom.
A fresh gentle breeze on a sunny day,
it has magical powers, many do say.

True, yes it's true, and so easy to find
if you submit thought to the delightful scene.
Dump worry and problem into the bin
to miss a moment, would be a sin.

You can walk up close to Flamborough Head,
its white chalk cliffs, from the beginning of time,
bearing a lighthouse, guiding those at sea,
with a bay giving shelter, from storm, in its lee.

Visiting beaches around the world, though never to compare,
the difference one finds, comes with age and time
now in the past, and with no more wish to roam,
Bridlington's the beach for me, lucky for me, it's home.

Maurice Wilkinson

SEPTEMBER 11TH 2001

. . . the day our world
        came to an end.
Sadness,
        a heaviness of spirit,
An inner stillness -
. . . dull edge of fear.
A cloud, obscuring thoughts
        of life and love,
A noonday darkness,
        covering all known things
No longer now
        as once they used to be.

Keep on, keep on.
Go on from strength to strength
Until again,
        a morning sun comes through.

Pettr Manson-Herrod

NOBODY LISTENS

To all drivers:
Every day I hear about some accidents you know,
Why is this? You may reply,
I simply do not know.
Is it simply tiredness or is it the wife,
We must put a stop to this
And try to get things right.
I know you do long journeys
To Scotland or Penzance.
You must be fit, not tired
I think you'll understand.
Think of home and your family
Keep this on your mind.
Watch out for others -
Never mind the time.
Then back home safely
To the family and wife,
Keep on driving, and stay alive.

Rolo

WITH GOLD

The famous streets of London,
    So some said, were paved with gold.
There would Yorkie find freedom,
    Went there, when eighteen years old.
But soon he found no treasure,
    Tough restrictions he knew well,
His days were lacking pleasure
    Governed by a prison bell.
Then, for his father and mother,
    Did that sad young fellow yearn.
His course could be no other,
    On release, made his return.
Much tension on that journey,
    Was experienced by the lad,
Felt guilty and unworthy
    Of his faithful mum and dad.
But, on the train's arrival
    From which Yorkie did alight,
Were raised by two essential
    Arms of welcome in his sight.
He refound things that matter,
    Warmth and love, with constant care.
A feast was promised later,
    Mum's stew, apple pie to share.
Three stepped out from the station,
    Springtime glory did unfold.
Was all the Lord's creation,
    Walls of York, well lined with gold.

D J Price

THE FOREMAN

He scurried around the workshop, with his little fat ugly frame,
His bald head shines in the sunlight, as much as it does in the rain,
To everyone who knows him, he is a flaming pain,
His constant argy bargy, is driving us insane.

He creeps about the storehouse, every single day,
We wish he'd take his money, and bloody go away,
He hides down the racks, to jump out on our backs,
To try and catch us out, with his little fat hairy snout.

He walks with a stoop, and the hump on his back,
Is where he puts his awful hat,
If he reads this poem, I'll get the sack,
We all think, that he is a prat.

You can always tell where he has been,
Because the poisoned dwarf, turned all the lads mean,
To work with him, it is a sin,
The state this warehouse is now in.

So look around, when you pass by, if you look hard, you might just try,
To see the humpty back foreman of the factory,
With a little luck, he'll go away,
But don't hold your breath, or he'll dock your pay.

David Watkins

FRAGMENTED CITY
(BRADFORD'S CULTURE BID)

Like a mosaic,
Traditional and modern, blending,
Individually woven,
Cultures harmonious.

Freely moving,
In the fragmented city, lending,
Domes, spires, to minimalist blocks,
Creating dimensions.

J B Priestly,
Brontës, pop culture stars all sending,
Invitations to the tourist,
Art too, in Lister Park.

Fashion classics,
Styles for all types encourage spending,
Such a variety of food,
Counter or table served.

Drama and dance,
'Bradford Bulls' stamping ground defending,
Technology, science and sport,
With leisure industries.

City of hope,
Bright futures arising, unending,
Preserving cultures with kindness,
But streetwise tolerance.

__Kathleen Mary Scatchard__

A PIECE OF ENGLAND

The green hills and valleys of West Yorkshire
Were once covered in a hazy mist,
Of smoke from mill chimneys and house fires,
We were unaware of what we missed.

Sturdy stone walls and buildings,
These features were built to last.
They serve as a reminder of our heritage
May we always value the good from the past.

The wild Yorkshire moors invite us to visit
To take in deep breaths of clean, fresh air,
Spiky, golden gorse bushes, purple heather,
and coarse green grasses.
Where the sheep wander, like moving grey boulders
without a care.

Looking down on the town from the top of a hill,
Now we are smokeless, it's all so clear.
The churches, the Town Hall, the markets and the
Piece Hall,
Are foundations, treasures and pleasures
for all who are here.

Kathleen McBurney

TIME

Where has all the time gone
Did you hear it whisper through the grass?
Perhaps as ragged clouds sail by
Hold the minutes as they pass

Time passed too quickly when dancing
All those years ago
Yet then I didn't notice
Inside me, such a glow

So this is life, time moving on
Living, then blessed sleeping through the night
Using your allotted span of years -
For *Time* is infinite!

Barbara Robson

COUNTRY CRICKET

Colonel Stanyforth of Kirk Hamerton Hall
Loved cricket with all his heart
Took his team to West Indies
Always one to take part
Back home he had constructed
A cricket pitch in the park
With a glorious rural setting
Even a miniature lake
On cool summer evenings
The villagers used to come
To watch their local heroes
In their attempts for runs
A quieter life a gentler one
Simpler pleasures then
We seem to have lost the art now
Never to come again
The ground has been re-located
Perhaps the game has too
All baseball caps and colourful sweats
With music as a background
Is nostalgia all we have left.

Barbara Williams

BYGONES

In Grandma's button box we find -
Bygones of a gentle kind.
A bone handled bodkin, a crochet hook,
If I had time I could write a book.
Linen buttons made for washing
I wonder - would they stand the bashing
Of a modern automatic?

Mother of pearl buttons, what a beautiful name
I remember the coat from which they came,
Soft brown velvet, warm and friendly
Worn by mother each weekend -
I can still feel its texture against my cheek
As from behind her skirts we used to peek
As she stopped to talk with a friend.

There are bygone tools in Grandpa's attic,
All hand powered, non-automatic,
A whet stone for sharpening, an old brace and bit
Each needing patience, bringing sweat to the brow.
If I close my eyes I can picture him now.

As the saying goes - 'let bygones be bygones'
When you reach our age, it is good to rely on
A kettle that boils at the touch of a knob
But it doesn't sing like Grandma's did
Bubbling away on the hob.

Constance Vera Dewdney

GLOBAL WARMING! ARMAGEDDON?

In Yorkshire within the year two thousand
In the autumn of that year, the rains
They were in deluge, lasting days and nights,
And into weeks I fear, flooding fields and villages
It burst the banks of rivers, including the River Aire.
Nor was the Ouse so friendly,
Inhabitants of York in fear,
For the steps that they had taken,
Flood barriers built last year,
Proved of slight protection, their failure now was clear.
Water, water everywhere, three to four foot deep,
Everywhere was flooded, for some no place to sleep!
The damage to their houses made many people weep,
Whilst the rising of the River Aire did up to bedrooms creep.
And flooded fields and countryside, were looking more like lakes,
Quite deep! It brought disaster, to farm animals and sheep.
For years some sources had been telling us
That a problem there would be, for the atmosphere,
Environment, was warming up, you see!
They blamed it on global warming, but,
When it came to explanation, no one
Seemed quite clear, so we all laughed,
It's just a joke, there's now't for us to fear!
And that's the way we viewed it, that's how it did appear!
But now we start to wonder, for the flooding
Brings no cheer, have we been too nonchalant,
Is Armageddon getting near?

Bah Kaffir

HOME THOUGHTS FROM HOME

Yorkshire! We, your folk, still hail thee,
Fairest soil, broad acres too.
White Rose County, once so mighty,
Our Father's earth on us endue.

Once so grand with all your power,
With your produce serving all.
Gone now is your finest hour
Of your hey-day past recall.

Coal and steel no longer needed,
Heavy woollens gone the same.
Fish stocks from our ports depleted,
Cries of sale are all in vain.

Cathedrals, castles are still with us,
Moorland, dales and wolds galore.
Produce now all sharply withers,
Cheaper still from Singapore.

And still the Brontë sisters beckon
To all travellers passing by.
Ilkley Moor bah't'at I reckon
Stays with us not yet to die.

Come, feast yourselves on Yorkshire pud,
And top it off with Wensley's cheese,
And this with Yorkshire ale I would
Not ask for owt as fine as these.

Charles Holmes

A Visit To Wentworth In March 2002

We touched the twisted lover's knot, and opened up the gate.
The long path stretched before us, past pleasures lay in wait.
Slowly as we wandered, along the flower filled lane,
The drab cold days of winter, slowly fell away.
Spring awakened from her sleep, reached out her gentle arms
Entwined us oh so tenderly, in her tranquil throes.
Daffodils softly beckoning, led us to Paradise Row.

Once more we tasted nature's wine, intoxicating nectar
Wrapped in the garb of yester-year we viewed the past with pleasure.
The old stone church, for centuries stood fast upon this place,
Cottages with green tiled roofs, mossily asleep.
A timeless air, of laisser-faire, a glimpse of days gone by.
Here in this place so far away, a feeling of peace and calm.
The past restored we felt again, the touch of the season's warmth.

Lyn Wilkinson

Listen To The Silence

Listen to the silence
There's a lesson to be heard,
It's coming down from Heaven
It's calling the living word,
You can feel it the air
It's in every breath you breathe,
You could touch the face of Jesus
If only you'd receive,
He is kneeling down and praying
And his heart is broke in two,
His thoughts are in the silence
He created just for you.

Jack Birkhead

THE FIVE SEASONS

Autumn, season of mists and bitter fruitlessness.
Damp leaves litter my path to the chemist's
My music becomes more mournful
I stay in bed longer

Winter brings flashes of frost,
Our one family dinner of the year,
And other, more painful, shared experiences.
Alcohol and brain cells engage in chemical warfare.
I join another gym
And stay in bed longer

Spring, and a young man's thoughts
Turn to fiendish, subcontinental wrist spinners,
Freshness,
And wearing less in bed.
Whilst sleeping longer.

Now is the summer,
Hemlines raise interest and possibilities
But the fruitlessness still tastes bitter.
Marlboro and Parkins sell out
But there is always banana milk.
I stay in bed late.

A long, thin season
Threads its way through
Frost, freshness, mists and maybes.
A constancy of a different coldness.
A silent season
That makes me want to sleep
Each time I wake the same.

David Parker

Welder Am I

As a welder I stand alone,
    Surrounded by fumes and an alien blue glow
Working all day this way
    People come and go, some stay and chat
But as a welder I stand alone,
    Time is my enemy, he lets me think in my blue glow
Go this way, go that way, say this or maybe that
    Care for a chat with my enemy and me
I find I can put the world to rights, or wrong
    Amidst the fumes and smog
My eyes they watch the molten blob as I weave away
    My mind, he's away
Go here, go there, do this, say that
    All this I do in my eerie blue glow
Today I weld away in Hawaii!

Kevin Dixon

MY 25P RISE

I've had my 80th birthday
I've reached the big '8 O'
I've had a rise in pension
So I'm ready for the big 'hey-ho'!
I went down to the post office
To collect my welcome rise
But when I reached the counter
I had a big surprise.
My mind was set on going abroad
But, deary, deary me
I found my great big wonderful rise
Wouldn't, buy me a cup of tea.

J Mary Kirkland

I Look In The Mirror And What Do I See?

I look in the mirror and what do I see?
An old, old woman, it's surely not me.
I turn my back on this old crone, leaving her there quite alone,
And in my mind I'm twenty-one with a handsome fella all my own.
At twenty-two I have a lad, the spittin' image of his dad.
The years roll by and eight years on, another lovely bouncing son,
Not like his dad but more like me, different in temperament you see.
We worked at our marriage and made it a go
A gift sent from Heaven to us here below.
We shared our few sorrows and lots of joys,
Going our way without too much noise,
Ignoring the jibes about Darby and Joan
We lived in a little world all our own
No thoughts of divorce (as couples now do)
Just plodding along like an old shoe.
A kiss in the morning, another at night and some in-between
To make it feel right, a quick 'I love you' and 'I love you too'
Seemed the natural thing to do.
I can't understand the modern way of living
Too much taking and not enough giving.
The sanctity of marriage gone forever,
No strong love to hold it together,
A little tiff and no 'Sorry dear, I didn't mean it' but 'Get out of here'.
So I think I'll return to the face in the glass
And tell her I'm sorry for being an ass
And reminisce there with a memory so clear
And remember my loved one, still ever near.

Emmie Tann

GROWING OLD

You know you're really getting old when
You're in the bath but can't get out again!
When you drop something on the floor
But picking it up makes your aching back sore.
When your shopping trolley is a great help you've found
To rest on - as you do your shopping round.
When you wait at a crossing for the all-clear
And a youngster comes up saying 'Can I help you across, dear'.
When a passing glance in a mirror mayhap
Shows your wrinkles resembling a busy road map.
When you're out for a day and it's not long before
You're looking around for a toilet door.
When your grandson says, 'Gran, want to get the feel of the 'mouse'
And your shrieks nearly raise the roof of your house,
When the dance band is playing a rousing jive
But you would prefer - to just 'take five'.
When at bedtime you should be climbing the stair
But you're forced to take that mobile chair.
But when great grandchildren call to see their great nan
You'll be glad of all the years you span
For when you look back over those years
With all their happiness and perhaps a few tears
All your memories you can unfold - so
How can they say 'there's nothing to growing old'.

Doreen Yewdall

SCARBOROUGH ROCK

The scenery is changing
In Scarborough's North Bay.
It once was sand and shingle,
Smooth pebbles and soft clay.

Now, it's like a building site,
And not a sight to see.
Huge barges and large boulders
Is all the eye can see.

To try to stop erosion -
As the cliffs are falling down -
They've filled the bay with rubble,
So the residents don't drown.

The rocks all come from Norway -
Transported overseas.
They should require a passport -
They're not in the EEC.

So, to return the compliment
And give Oslo quite a shock,
Why not redress the balance
And export Scarborough rock?

Brian M Wood

IT'S GORN

Is love supposed to end on a 47/48 bus
Was that all there was to us
Would I be entitled to cuss
Shouldn't it be a dramatic
Plunge over a cliff
Or on a Sheffield hospital bed
Cold and stiff
To the airs of a Mozart rift
That it is over
No doubt
But it couldn't have been
True (love)
Because I didn't scream and shout
Tell the world about
What is no more
Truth be known
Glad you no longer
Knock at my door.

G Stanley

Nature Play

Tiger-like
you wait
in silent watchfulness,
eyes alert
and fixed in steady gaze,
alert to every movement
from breeze-stirred grassy blade
to dew drop tremor on a leafy stem;
tiger-striped
your fragile face
with wide-eyed stare
is fierce in frantic expectation
of approaching prey;
what's that you see?
A bird
so feather-soft and tempting;
and from your shadowed forest
you lion-prowl on padded paws
emitting lance-sharp claws
in readiness to strike;
a moment's pause
with body held in rigid pose;
then
limbs quiver
as you gather
all reserves of strength
to launch yourself and pounce;
instant death
as claws pierce the warm soft body;
dripping droplets of blood
drip
drop
on the grass;
head severed:

rivulets of blood swift flow
on the grass;
lion-proud
you stalk away
with mouth-held victim,
limp and mangled,
hanging
drip
drop
red;
and on the grass a worm writhes:
the only sign,
a dying sign,
of the once live bird
now dead.

Margaret Ann Tait

WWW Dot Con

We sit in a cocoon of technology
    alone, contemplating not our navel
But the anatomy of science.
    We program in, record and print
Guided by codes and jargonese.
    This is not the world of actuality
No need to visit banks,
    to handle cash.
We transfer credit easily
    along the internet.
We look, we note, we buy.
    We sit in our swivel chairs
Commanding our little world.
    We map out journeys we may never take.
Access airports and hotels
    for weekend breaks.
Even order organic salmon
    from Scottish streams.
It would be better to surf real tides.
    To drive on narrow roads
Smelling the earthly air
    of fern filled moors,
To hear the curlews cry across the sky
    and watch the sun drown in the Western Isles.
But, locked in ethereal space
    we surf the air.
And world-wide webs
    arch clouded windows
Picking up dirt and bits and bytes of news
    along the way.
Are we the spiders in control
    or just trapped flies?

Olga M Momcilovic

SERGEANT PEPPER ENDS THE EMPIRE

Ghandi and Suez were wake up calls.
But the end of empire
Was truly brought home
On a sixties Saturday afternoon
When Mick McManus was body-slamming Jackie Pallo,
And father was moulding bait from stale 'Mother's Pride'.

My brother,
Dandy/anarchist by nature, came home,
Proud as punch, by the front door,
With a shocking red guard's tunic.
Gold epaulettes shimmered.
Brass buttons stood out like ceiling bosses.
Red and blue braiding criss-crossed the breast.

Father, apoplectic, engaged him.
This was the Rourkes Drift,
The rearguard action of a generation.
While he could tell you everything about Napier at Plessey,
Gordon of Khartoum,
He knew nothing of Sergeant Pepper,
Preferred the '1812' to Captain Beefheart.
My attention was half-Nelsoned
'Til the garden gate was slammed.

Confectionery soldiers are no match for real ones.
My brother was made to take it back.

Later that afternoon,
He returned
(By the back door)
With yellow tartan hipsters.

Peter Ardern

TRASH

The heat's haze was rising,
From the dry, pale pavement,
So hot that he was gasping,
Grasping the cold can of pop.
The coolness flowed delightfully down,
The most refreshing drink ever drunk,
It had never tasted so good,
Been so necessary for health,

For without that drink he would have died,
Or so he thought, finishing fastly.
Then crushed it, destroyed it, mangled,
Angled beyond recognition.
Deformed and horrible, it was slung,
An egotistical strongman's act,
Using brawn not brains, not even common-sense,
Tossing the unwanted away, anywhere.

It was left littering the park,
Unnoticed and unwanted junk,
Until the soft sweet scent blows in the wind,
Determined he stalks it like the pheasant,
Paws it and throws it, running after,
Again and again, a makeshift ball,
He's chewing it even more. 'Yelp.' The sharp point stabs.
He backs off, leaves it not knowing better, he's hurt.

Laughing, playing children run and roll,
Falling happily down the grass bank,
Spongy, soft, safe green mattress,
What a mess? Cuttings in hair.
Football, races, tig, catch . . . scratch, tears
Trickle like the blood from the knee.
It's there again, edges pointing, metal gleaming.
The kid limps away, not thinking to make it safe.

On such a nice day the park is busy,
Bikers, picnikers and sweaty joggers,
The sparkle of the can catches their eye,
As passers-by stop to see what they've found.
Some money, a sparkling diamond perhaps,
Or a trinket, the magpies swoop to seize,
'Ah, it's just an old can never mind,'
And they leave it, they didn't do it.

So tiny and yet so dangerous,
Multiplied over our roads and parks,
As empty, hungry bins wait,
Anticipate the rubbish.
Recycling bins yell out for more nourishment,
Crying for aluminium and paper,
But why bother? Let them starve, it's not our problem,
Until the trees have gone and species are extinct.

Karen Cawthorn

THE ADDICTION

Life has changed
Changed so much for me
No longer are you foremost in my mind
Easing my pain when you're here
Kissing you, my lips on fire for you
My body aching for you
No longer am I raging mad when you're away
No longer do you rule my day
Life has changed
Changed so much for me
No longer do you wear me out
Make me out of breath when you're about
So frightened you'll run out on me
And I'll pace the floor in agony
You took my life before it began
Made me your slave, your innocent fan
You deceived me and made me depend on you
For courage and power and precedence too
You made me think I needed you
That I couldn't function without you
What a fool I happened to be
For years and years you hoodwinked me
I never believed I could feel so at peace
So calm and serene and secure
I never believed I had a choice
And that when you were gone, I'd rejoice
I can sleep through the night
And not care if you're not there in the morning light
To satisfy my ever-burning desire
And refuel my never-ending fire.

Life has changed
Changed so much for me
Freedom has come back to me
No longer do you dictate where I go
Or how long I can stay
I make my own decisions now
I stopped smoking
 . . . that wonderful day.

Karen A Neville

HICKORY DICKORY DOCK
AT PENISTONE MARKET TOWN

Penistonians for months have been as puzzled as can be
For every time they pass the church it's twenty five past three;
'For Heaven's sake' they cry in vain, 'have mice climbed
                                                 up the steeple?'
There's something sadly wrong to cause such chaos to our people.
'Let's ask the mayor' a wise man spoke, 'he'll know just what to do'
But he's busy reading 'minutes' and that takes 'hours' too.
'So how about the vicar - he'll know the reason why'
But he'll have to ask the Bishop who will answer with a sigh:
'What - dip into our coffers - nay, with time you'll have to cope'
So there's just one more suggestion - we'll have to ask the Pope!
But the Pope is having to revise the Sermon on the Mount
For the crowds who wait for 'hours' such a story to recount.
'Where are our lovely chimes' is all we ask of one accord?
Is Penistone not worthy - 'Surely' saith the Lord.

Margaret Marsh

A NAUGHTY BOY

Just wait till your dad gets home
My mother would say to me
He is sure to send you off to bed
And without your tea.

You've been climbing trees again
And have torn your new shirt
And by the state of your clothes
You've been playing in the dirt.

You will cop it this time my lad
When I tell him what you've done
For I've had to do your chores
Whilst you've been out having fun.

Now go and get into the bath
And wash behind those ears
For it's no use sulking now my lad
So wipe away those tears.

If you tidy up your bedroom
And keep it nice and clean
I may forget to tell your dad
What a naughty boy you've been.

Victor Brunt

GREEN VALLEY

It wasn't death, but the earth itself
that filled his lungs with dust
and left the blue-black scars
across the weakened hands

among the fossils
where no man should work
a diamond core, black and hard
was hewn from the seams of his mind

fourteen,
he worked beside the door
to vent the capillaries
of the sculpted serpent's lungs

among the fossils
where no man should work
he wiped away the sweat
and stoked the glowing embers of his dreams

twenty,
he stood among the men
who sang in hymns to the lift's descent
and cheered with the siren's blast

among the fossils
where no man should work
the trickling thoughts sprang up
and the ember glow was red

thirty and wise
the hardened core
of this diamond mind
blew off its dusty sheath

among the fossils
where no man should work
a shining hammer
from the ember glow was smelt

and a leader stood
to face the wrath
of those who would
enslave his work

*among the fossils
where no man should work
a curved blade raised its gleam
from the belly of the hungry hill*

*among the fossils
a thought was one day sprung that
blackened valleys would again be green*

*among the fossils
lie the sleeping hopes of those
who dreamt this world could grow*

*among the fossils
cry the dusty tears
of those who lived
for fair and just return*

and greening hills forget

that no man
should by others' freedom
be enchained

nor to others' gain
should his value be denied.

Ruth Kavanagh

Anno Domini

This morning, feeling rather smart
in flowery skirt and matching top
I chanced upon a care worker who spoke to me
'I just live there, if 'ere you need
to ask for help . . .'

Well - look at me, my hair is grey
yet so was hers, perhaps with help
and not like mine which naturally
grew that way.

When did this feeling first begin?
I don't know, I used to be thin!
But now the sizes seem to grow
and all my bumps begin to show.

My feet, they itch, and start to swell
the joints all ache, and twinge as well.
My singing voice folk did applaud
now often produces a harmonic chord.

The bus driver never seems to ask
'Please may I see your bus pass?'
Perhaps it's better not to be seen
for the picture there shows my hair green!

I fill my days with things to do,
artistic, creative, helpful too.
I try to sing, to draw and paint -
but Constable is what I ain't.

Am I old? May be in part . . .
But inside I'm very
Young at heart!

Marjorie Upson

THE SEA

Up from its bed the sea comes a-roaring
White foaming wrath it sends a-pouring.
Dashing with fury against the sea wall
Like some gasping monster it rises and falls.
Crashing and lashing it snaps at the shore
Continually turning it comes back for more.
Rearing and veering all creatures it mocks
Snapping and snarling its way through the rocks.
Ships toss and turn within its great jaws
Battered and creaking they slip from its claws.
Then worn out and weary it finally sinks.
Down onto its bed it calmly slinks.

E D Stevenson

The Master Plan

When the Creator made the world,
The heaven, the earth, the sea,
With care He made each living thing,
Fish, animals, and birds to sing.
The trees and flowers, each in their place,
And last of all the human race.
Our God, He had a master plan,
And finished His great work with man.

Now many thousand years have rolled
Since first the world was made,
And it ran smoothly by God's plan
As He created it for man.
For each and every living thing,
From animals to birds that sing,
To everything a place was given
From master plans made up in Heaven.

But somehow it has all gone wrong,
I think you will agree,
That chaos now begins to reign.
It really has become quite plain
That we have lost our sense of place,
All creatures, and the human race,
And difficulties do begin
For every single living thing.

It isn't what the Master planned
When first the world He made.
The greed, the wars, and land made waste,
Starvation for the human race.
But violence and corruption came,
And man, not God must take the blame.
The evil lust for power and might
Took over. Men began to fight.

It's not too late to make amends
If seeds of love are sown.
The nation's leaders must agree.
God must again the Master be.
Then like a snowdrop in the spring
The seeds will grow, and once again
We'll see God had a master plan
To save the world, He made the man.

Barbara Dunning

RETIREMENT

Retirement comes to one and all yes it affects someone every day
To think about retirement does not come easy it seems oh so far away
What must go through one's mind when one has to take a final bow
No more to say good morning and to use all that old know how
Some people will pat you on the back and show some kind of smile
Yet while wishing you all the best really they hate your style
After retirement time may lay heavy on your hands even on your mind
But now time for friends is abundant and lots more friends you'll find
You're missed for a while by some but to others you'll
                                          always be around
You're not being seen or heard to some makes silence an unusual sound
Work was a challenge you faced every day retirement a new
                                          challenge to meet
Don't be afraid of retirement think only of the world now
                                          laid at your feet.

Bob T

LUNCH ALFRESCO

The garden umbrella covered me
Shading me from the sun's glare.
Lunching at my table
I suddenly became aware
Of a bee drowsily buzzing
Way above my head.
Rambling from rose and honeysuckle
On the cotton flowerbed.

I watched it search for nectar
Persistently bumbling around,
Beguiled by the colourful canopy
In my garden where flowers abound.

I kept on glancing up there
The droning and the heat
Tired me before the bee did
And I dozed there on my seat.

A silence and I raised my head
Vexed to find it gone
I'd missed its flight away
But the memory lingers on.

Pauline Boncey

RETIREMENT

Some save through trouble and strife,
To prepare for the ultimate perfect life.
A life with money enough to enjoy.
No more work! Oh boy!
Just be sure there is money enough in the bank.
They will have the shares and pensions to thank.

Nothing is ever the same on the other side of the fence.
I have been here a while. There is no trouble with pence!
With arthritis and diabetes to mention a few.
A great jab, to prevent the onset of flu.
Eyes need testing; the teeth are also going.
Thank goodness for the fuel bonus, when it is snowing.

I try to explain to the young, how fast time flies.
With grey hair on top, they think I mix the truth with lies.
Every moment is precious! Make it count.
Value what you have and let the memories mount.
Now we have time to appreciate how many good things are free.
So enjoy the anticipation of retirement.
It was the best part for me!

Mary Parker

FRIDAY NIGHT AT PARAGON STATION

Blue buses weave continually in and out
Belching exhaust fumes
As the station begins to crowd with people
Out to enjoy Friday night
Celebrate the end of another week with their latest wages.

Teenage girls in short skirts, sleeveless tops
Bare legs and platform shoes, no coats
Crowd together waiting for dates and each other.

Students in jeans and bomber jackets struggle with heavy rucksacks
Making their way to the railway station
To visit friends and families for their weekend away from Hull.

Acned adolescent boys approaching manhood shout catcalls
At older women anxious to go home
Away from the raucousness
Of Friday nights
Congregate uneasily on graffitied platforms
Littered with cigarette butts and discarded tickets.

Easing off as the pubs begin to fill
The vendor shuts up shop, quietness takes over
By nine o'clock hardly a soul about
Just a tramp lumbering with all his worldly goods in plastic carrier bags
Sits on the steps of a closed booking office to drink his meths.

Eleven o'clock, pubs have emptied and drunk humanity
Shouting and jeering spills out into the station
Trying to frantically catch the last bus
Leaving the sense of fear for those not drunk
Shrink into the platform walls, hoping not to draw attention.

Last buses return, everything closes up for the night
Quietness settles over Paragon Station
Only to be broken by the noise of people lining up for taxis.

Marie Housam

PLAYING THE CARDS GIVEN

When perfection has missed its curtain call
Someone suffers, but most, not at all
In life we see the mistakes every day
There's no discount on offer, the bill says pay.
Alone in a room we know who we are
A mirror that lies kindly hides the scar,
People are everywhere but nobody's near
What's going for us is that we're still here.

Bill Warby

THE OLD MILL TOWN

I do not love my Yorkshire town
In fact I hate it sorely
I go sometimes and gaze around
And truly come home poorly

The Town Hall Square - memorial of those dead in the war
'Lest we forget', well, they've done that, and all that went before

Brave soldiers, sailors, and airmen killed
All the blood and tears that spilled
It cuts me to the core

Because they held a barbecue
The square was filled with sundry stalls
The stink of burgers sizzling, raucous shouts and calls
Onions fried, rap music blared and everyone had a laugh
While all the unkempt, scruffy kids, climbed up the Cenotaph!

At great expense, a company built a fine and smart Bus Station
State of the art technology, so comfortable and clean
But now you see it thronged with folks and their relations
Dotted with chewing gum, the elegant paving
Muddy trainers on seats of teenagers raving
How magnificent it had been

No, I don't love my Yorkshire town
With its ignorant, ill-tempered masses
Greedy, no manners, self-centred and rude
Spilling their curries and other fast food
Lurching and swearing and acting the fool
Not knowing respect that once was the rule
Of the proud Yorkshire working classes.

Disillusioned

SUMMER AFTERNOON AT OTLEY

Glossy green turtles, pink marbled mice
Shiny paper bags, filled when they go.
My sons choose at the sweet shop
From a violent e-numbered rainbow.

White with dark rudders at the rear
Like fish on a black granite slab
Swans glide
In raindrop pock-marked water by the weir.

Cracked concrete crazy golf
With escape routes for the rain;
The rivulets roll better than my aim
But the gap-toothed smile for the score just won
Lets me know my day was a hole in one.

Deborah Tuddenham

THE FLOOD

The curtains are closed,
It's dark in here,
All I hear is the rain on the window,
The wind in the trees
And the birds as they fly.
I remember now,
The year of the flood,
When,
John was killed,
The church fell,
The land was gone and the sea was all.
The people, few,
In boats and on odd islands
The roofs were gone, too the traffic.
Yes, I remember it well,
A terrible year for rain.
The rain's stopping now.
If only, those years ago,
It could have stopped too,
Poor John,

One day the rain will come and stay for good,
Oh Lord,
Let there never be another flood.

Catherine Day

INDUSTRIAL SURVIVAL

Britain was once an industrial nation,
Shipbuilding and steel assisted our salvation;
Chemical and engineering, both dominant in their field,
Helped to improve exports, with a percentage high yield.

The computer age with modern terminology,
Has brought about advanced technology;
Work forces in industry are being depleted,
Throughout the world, the story is repeated.

Our fishing industries have reached stagnation,
Some farmers and hauliers are close to resignation;
Petrol and diesel prices have reached a record high,
Whilst the taxes and duties, ensure the chancellor gets by.

Foreign imports are rising fast,
Hopefully this situation will not last;
Companies abroad are very repetitive,
Our survival depends on being competitive.

All of our work forces are part of a team,
Pulling together and full of esteem;
Constantly striving to improve the output,
As their company's future, depends on their input.

Inefficiency can lead to orders being lost,
Small companies can't always recover the cost;
Study the problem, don't suffer the pain,
Loyalty to customers will not be in vain.

Bring any problems to the management's attention,
No matter how trivial, they deserve a mention;
Some duplicate paperwork is ineffective,
Saving on despatches is now cost effective.

Producing products which are high in demand,
Can result in companies needing to expand;
Skilled labour is available to ensure we succeed,
Targets for industry, Britain can certainly exceed.

Malcolm Goat

THOUGHTS

I know it's only a picture card
But the beauty is there to see
Imagine if it came to life
How glorious that would be
The air would be filled with scent of sweet flowers
The rustle of the wind through the trees, tall like towers
Children's eyes all agleam
On the old wooden bridge overlooking the stream
They have just seen a fish to their delight
Made their day perfect made it just right
And it's been so nice for me to stay
In that wonderful wood so far away
So you see a picture card has its appeal
When you dream on and make it feel real.

K M Parker

FEEDING THE PAIN

His mother whom he adored had abandoned him,
gone to live with her new lover called Tim,
oh? why did she do it when he loved her so
his dad was alright, but he didn't understand his ways,
how was he going to manage without her but crying won't help,
so William decided to go and find her, plead her to come home
as she was needed, here all the more,
he had just entered his teens and missed her so,
so William crept out one dark night, quietly shutting the door
he'd saved his pocket money, and took some cash from
his father's pocket while he was sleeping,
but alas he was waylaid in his search, by a drug addict
promising he'd help him, and introduced him to drugs,
which made him forget about his mother, of which he stole
and abused people to feed his addiction,
while his father blamed himself for letting his wife go
and worried about his son he phoned the police,
the police searched in vain to find where he laid,
but in the end he killed for money of which he paid
the police found his body strung up in his room of an
old disused building which the police had missed,
William had committed suicide because of the pain,
his father managed to find his mother, who was nearly insane
for her lover had left her to seek another mistress,
but his dad took her back again because of the trauma
of their son, forgiving her the trouble she'd caused,
as the coffin was lowered into his grave his mother
tearfully threw a bunch of red roses onto his coffin
blowing kisses, wishing she hadn't left him for a wasted
few months of love, but one cannot turn the clock back
because of one's folly, shame enveloped her as she looked at Jack.
The couple then turned away from him hand in hand
William's smiling apparition watching them go
A big white dove sat on his shoulder.

M J Chadwick

DRUGS

His appearance sparked off a lot of joy.
He held her hand against the pain.
Their desire in life had been fulfilled.
Happiness beyond their wildest dreams.
The waiting, planning, praying was stilled.
And as the tears flowed their son was born.
He grew up through his childhood days.
And was looked upon with pride.
His modest achievements exalted them.
With sheer joy they could not hide.
But through the door of life he sees.
The evil, the lust, the avarice, the hate.
The choice is yours the good voice calls.
Choose with care before it's too late.
The skin pierced by needle pricks.
The cheap and squalid back rooms.
To ride a chariot up into the sky.
The perfect journey to space.
All the fascinating colour vanquished and lost.
No stress, no care, no race.
The symbol, the key to open the door.
To banish restraint, and cruel thoughts.
A ride that is not really sane.
When they found out, they wanted to cover it up.
Denied that he was part of the scene.
Screamed that it was a lie, a lie.
Even hoped that it was all a dream.
As sadly each asked, for God's sake why.
He in turn had no remorse.
Lay the blame at his forefathers' door.
The dole queues, inflation, rejection, the cost.
The crushing eventuality of war.
Parents regret, such was the shame.
The violence that exploded their hopes all torn.
Now only the debris lay at their feet.

And regret that he had ever been born.
Slowly the dawn of truth.
The ever recurring vision was seen.
The spray of flowers, the fresh turned earth.
A gravestone inscription, what did it mean.
It took time to penetrate the drug filled brain.
But when it did the fight was on.
The couple once happy to see him born.
Prayed and cried for their only son.
People without trouble are dead.
God give this boy trouble, we want him to live.

K Ainsley

CATCHING GAMES

In a doorway, Ian halted
to let me through, and my world faltered
a New Boy in his uniform
who smiled at me that sunny morn

I bet he felt the way I did,
that eager bright-eyed playful kid;
to make me join in chasing fun,
he'd call me names, then laugh and run

I wish those days would never end
capturing my playground friend
Our boyhood catching games, you see
meant holding him in front of me

How I loved to feel him struggle,
my kneesock'd mate who teased and tussled
His ticklish body and cheeky face
would writhe and plead in my embrace

'You've caught me, you Bulldog!' Ian cried,
his arms now pinned down by his sides
I stood behind and held him tight
he wriggled, but he couldn't fight!

'I've got you, Prisoner!' I confirmed,
my gleeful captive bucked and squirmed
Our locked young bodies toppled over
to wrestle on the summer clover

The brightest star in all of space
could not outshine his smiling face
and now I'd love to see once more,
the childhood friend that I adored

We're tangled still, but in my dreams;
he's gone, and life feels incomplete . . .
schoolmates leave, and fade with time
though he could never leave my mind.

Charlie Duffin

Summer's Gone

The leaves are brown
And tinged with gold
And all the flowers
Are growing old

The colour green is fading fast
The summer's been
It didn't last

The snow will come
Then all too soon
All we'll see
Is a frosty moon

The sky will fill
With darkest night
Oh how I long
For summer bright.

H Matthews

ONE SUMMER'S DAY

The leaves dance vibrantly, in the gentle summer breeze
As the waves on the lake
Lapping softly on the shingle
With the waterfall cascading
And the hollyhocks stretching high into the sky
And the perfumed air
Sets your senses on fire.

With your hand in mine
We walk through the painted landscape
Heading towards the ivy covered cottage
Where roses the colours of the rainbow
Twist and turn over the doorway
And under the window and through the arch.

The yellow and the orange of the marigolds
The pinks and reds of the salvias mingle with
And intertwine with the pendulum branches of the fuchsias
Laden heavily with dancing ballerinas
And walking along the old stone path
The lemon scented thyme rises from beneath our feet
Your hand brushes through the lavender sending
Waves upon waves of its everlasting bouquet
Throughout the rest of the garden.

With your hand in mine as we sit on the old rustic bench
Running your fingers through the branches of rosemary
Lovingly watching the bees take the nectar
From the pink jasmine
And the Mexican orange blossom intoxicating the senses
The cornflowers around our feet bobbing and swaying
In the sweet scented air we kiss . . .
Then we say goodbye.

C F Hauxwell

THE PRINCE OF THE LONELY NIGHT

As the sun sinks low behind snow-capped mountains,
Dark, shady shadows slip round the corner of the door.
His robes of satin leave a path of sorrow and misery,
His bony fingers, long and thin, leave a cobweb of eternal
Nightmares hanging over you.

Expressionless eyes and thin blue lips
Look down upon you from beneath a
Concealing hood, with hanging silver hair, star-like,
Wrapping you in a blanket of darkness.
Taking away the sight of your bedroom.

Spreading terror over the surface of the world
The nightmares sink into your head!
Bewitching your mind, your body, your soul!
The world is in cold darkness, nightmare-full,
He smothers you. Fear and horror fills your heart!

His home of rock, mountain caves,
Are hatred full, empty of possession.
The arrival destroys peace of mind
For all the animals,
The Prince of the Lonely Night.

Emma Warwick (11)

CHANGING SEASONS

They walked in the footsteps
Of the men in front, on the bitter
Winter's days, them, like ghosts
Not making new prints
In the softly laid snow

Like devils in disguise, they
Brought about a path through the Baltic
Conditions which stuck through the
Spring and into the summer turned
Into a bustling cobbled street

And then came autumn leaves
And a change of scene
For a group of young men
Who left the cobblestone streets
For the surrounding woods of ignorance
With wooden wheels
Rattling beneath their feet

They returned, it was said
To the spring sun

With air beneath their feet
And wings by their sides.

Christopher Philpott

HATS

Assuming different roles in life
Many hats we wear
Some we flaunt
Some we lose
Some we gladly share

Sensible, wide brimmed and chic
A mother's hat
Will firmly stick
Through varied parts
She must enact
To keep her family safe, intact

When she discards this tight chapeau
Her hair is flowing free
New windmills she'll demolish
To gain her own identity

Provider, confidante and guide
A father's hat is worn with pride
Sometimes it slips
With undue strain
Hope re-adjusts its style again

Crushed Panamas
Hide precious dreams
Of avenues unexplored
School caps tucked in satchels
Give way to mortar boards

Worn with panache and confidence
Most hats will see us through
The rigours of life's journey
As new adventures we pursue.

Eveline Weighell

GLIMPSES OF HEAVEN

A baby's smile a favourite song
Being part of a family knowing you belong,
The sun breaking through clouds of grey
Rays of gold to brighten the day.
A blackbird carolling its evening hymn
The delicate colours of the butterfly's wing.
Northern lights that seem to shimmer and fly
Shades of paradise painting the sky,
Words of love that speak to your soul
Glimpses of Heaven more precious than gold.

Mazard Hunter

SILHOUETTES

Pale moonlight, dusky sky
Silhouettes of darkness play tricks on my eye

Watching the tide in the still of night
A line of white hands to the shore cling tight

You are wild, passionate, serene then calm
Pounding away mainland with mighty arm

Hidden depths no eye can see
Your secret of life is eternity

I watch you over rocks as hurriedly you rush
Whispering a lullaby in chorus you whoosh!

Maureen Gilbert

A Mother's Farewell

A breathless pause, a tiny scream,
Is the answer to my dreams,
A little girl or little boy
Is here at last to bring me joy,
I've forgotten the pain, the discomfort too,
It was worth it all, just for you.
Through teething tears and happy smiles
My baby grows before my eyes.
A toddler small, then a schoolchild tall,
To love and cherish through it all,
Hopes and ambitions shining bright,
I only hope I can guide you right,
Schooldays gone, you're an adult at last,
With your way to make helped by your past,
Romance blooms, true love is near
The day is close when you will not be here,
Today is your wedding day my dear,
I'll try hard not to shed a tear
From the start I knew you were only lent
With another the rest of your life would be spent,
May you have the happiness you deserve,
And God bless and help you, through the years.

M G Clements

WHEN DOES ROMANCE END?

When does romance finally end?
When does romance finally go?
Does it end all at once or
Does it creep up on us,
Bit by bit, kinda slow?

When do we stop buying her flowers?
When do we stop buying her chocolates and sweets?
And when do we stop holding hands
When out walking in the streets?

When do we stop being kind?
When do we stop opening doors?
When do we start thinking, what's mine is mine
Instead of, what's mine is yours?

When do we start getting selfish?
When do we stop thinking of sharing?
When do we actually start losing interest?
When do we actually stop even caring?

Who knows when romance finally ends.
Just when, why, where or how.
And when do we become so bored by it all
That we can't even be bothered to row?

But remember,
There's always a chance,
You might just save a romance.
Start looking for the good points.
Stop looking for the flaws.
Start being kind again.
Start opening those doors.
And with luck,
The romance that you save,
Could well be yours.

David Sim

NICKEY'S YEAR

You stole into my life when abandoned and small,
Frightened, unsure, not trusting a soul.
September it was when leaves turned to gold,
You chased them all day till the nights turned cold.

The winter descended with ice cold winds, snow lying soft and deep,
Your lovely green eyes showed trust at last and daily, a visit
                                                   you'd keep.
I fed you and loved you and watched you grow,
Stronger and lovelier than ever before.

Came your first spring while you basked in the sun,
You would purr and give pleasure in all your found fun.
Chasing butterflies was your favourite game, looking at ladybirds crawl.
In the garden you found such a world of peace
'Neath the flowers and hedges so tall.

Barely a year you spent with me, when the good Lord took you away,
Oh Nickey, Nickey, I loved you so and miss you day by day.

The garden is empty and quiet now,
Your presence is no longer here.
Are you still chasing butterflies in God's garden perhaps?
While I helplessly shed a tear.

Jean Naseby

A Housewife's Work Is Never Done

While washing breakfast dishes I think out loud.
Oh the joys of a housewife, reluctantly houseproud.
Does anyone notice those mundane chores?
Dutifully performed by 'her indoors'.

Who removes the grime from the toilet bowl,
Cleans the dirt from a muddy boot's sole.
Hoovers daily, dusts and more,
Washing windows, cleaning floors.

Empties rubbish from the waste bins
Cleans kitchen cupboards, rearranging tins.
Wipes kitchen units inside and out.
We can't have grease and grime about.

Ah, another load of washing's done,
It's time to switch the iron on.
Soon there's piles of clothes to put away,
Then sew the hem that's started to fray.

Check the clock - it's time for school
Collect the kids then off to the pool.
Back home in time to cook the tea.
Oh no -
More dirty dishes for me!

Tracey Ibbotson

THE DISAPPEARING LOOS OF CLEVELAND

On Coatham prom where hundreds pay to stay
and children on the beaches play,
the graffiti declares they are free
but obviously there's nowhere to spend a penee!
the disappearing loos of Cleveland

In Lock Park I thought there would be a chance
but with crossed legs I could see at a glance,
though kiddies played and ducks did lark
the doors were locked well before dark,
the disappearing loos of Cleveland

In Saltburn Square at three
you have to go behind a tree.
How did we get in such a state?
With hundreds rattling at the gate,
the disappearing loos of Cleveland

At North Skelton they used to be fine
but now houses stand in a line,
in Lingdale they stood for years in disrepair
you've guessed now they are not even there,
the disappearing loos of Cleveland.

In this county where tourists flock
they are all due a rude awakening shock.
They will all declare this is not funny
we will go elsewhere to spend our money,
the disappearing loos of Cleveland.

What will happen in the end
if this becomes a national trend.
Trained gangs of poopa-scooping dogs
lamenting the demise of the British public bogs,
the disappearing loos of Cleveland.

David Burton

OFF TO LONDON

On Sunday night the alarm was set,
It did not go off just yet,
It went off at five past six on Tuesday night
Giving Janet a little fright,
For if we had awaited the alarm's ring for Monday,
The purple clock would have a debt to pay.
For Monday was a trip to London,
For both Janet and John.
Up and dressed by just gone 5 o'clock,
To the system this was a shock.
Breakfast and duties done,
Off to Darlington Railway Station before the sun.
The King's Cross GNER train arriving for half seven.
We might be functioning properly by eleven.
With speed up to 140 miles per hour, arriving from A to B
At journey's end Melissa I spotted, making us three.
The order of the day,
Is fast, forward, without delay.
Tubes, plates of meat and a red London bus,
Helped us bomb about the capital without fuss.
Chelsea where Melissa is a nanny is smart,
Of London a most select part.
The Houses of Parliament looking grand,
With Big Ben's big and little hand,
His time was coming up to half-past four,
The purple clock needs a lesson from him,
So the alarm does not function on a whim.
Piccadilly Circus with the moving adverts was fun,
Hope around here we can get a Chelsea bun.
Changing of the guard at St James' Palace,
Christopher Robin was not there with Alice.
For he goes to Buckingham Palace every day,
Including a July Monday
Hamley's toy shop in Regent Street,
Is where the young at heart meet.

Teddy bears galore, giraffes almost to the ceiling,
Lots on offer, everything appealing,
Carnaby Street was the place for John,
Here he tried a trendy cap on.
I never brought anything in the 60's we heard him say,
He purchased, without delay.
Walking over Westminster Bridge was a delight,
Old Father Thames a pleasing sight.
Fed and watered at McDonald's for tea,
Onward for John, Melissa and me.
To the Millennium Bridge, passing The London Eye,
A landmark reaching to the sky.
A quick look in the Tate Modern Gallery of Art,
It was a bit of a dart,
It was soon to close for the day,
We were having a busy Monday.
At Trafalgar Square, pigeons of three,
While being fed, landed on me.
They stood in a line on my left arm,
I did not come to any harm.
They ate my flapjack,
Some flew from the front and some from the back.
Throughout the day,
Melissa and Janet bought goods on the way.
A visit to London's China Town,
Was a treat to walk down.
The last stop for the day for us,
After getting off a London bus,
Was Covent Garden, where street entertainment was going on,
In an active part of London.
Here we had a drink in the Nag's Head and a rest,
We talked about what we had enjoyed best
We were getting to know our way around,
In a lift at Covent Garden, we went to the Underground,
The tube to King's Cross Station.

The favourite station of our nation,
The train for Newcastle at platform five,
Up North to Darlington it would arrive.
We thanked Melissa for a perfect day.
It had been worth it, getting up early on that Monday.

Janet Degnan

FAMILY TREASURES

Four precious grandkids who bring so much joy,
Three of them are beautiful girls -
The fourth, a handsome boy
So young, yet full of wisdom
They teach you so many things,
Their love is unconditional
No wonder my heart sings
Enjoy every moment
Be it gladness or pain
There may be little heartaches
But soon you'll smile again.
History repeats itself
And boy, am I glad
I think I've seen it all before
They're a copy of Mam and Dad.

Jean Lowe

THE GOOD OLD DAYS

They call them 'the good old days!'
A tin bath by the fire,
Layers of coal dust,
Air filled with fumes and smoke.
Tuberculosis.
Women weary with child-bearing,
Scrubbing, washing, cooking.
Never quite enough to eat.
Make-do and mend,
Throw nothing away.

But honour in society;
Help your neighbour;
Support the family;
Look after Grandma.
'Send a loaf to Peggy, her man can't work.'
Shops in villages selling everything under the sun.
Time to chat over the fence,
To look at the new baby,
To watch the dough rise.

Now we have acid rain,
The homeless in boxes,
SAM missiles, nuclear energy,
A throwaway society,
Adding to the rubbish mountain.
Indestructible plastic,
Frozen food.
Cancer.
This is our legacy to the next generation.
Stress, computers, whizz kids,
Shopping on Internet,
Teenage abortions, battered children,
Thieving and vandalism.

But no back-breaking toil.
Controlled pregnancies.
Equality for women?
Automatic washers, microwaves, vacuum cleaners.
Living in isolation in our own little houses,
Mortgage to pay, car to licence.

Were they the 'good old days'?

Jessica Ruggles

GUNPOWDER, TREASON AND PLOT

The days of waiting are all but over;
We're outside Ceddesfeld Hall.
Trees are weirdly silhouetted by
A yellow, haloed moon
Against a cloudless, dark sky;
A backcloth of shimmering, shiny stars.
Excited, expectant, chattering children;
The mingling smells of onions, soup and coffee.
Is that what Guy Fawkes had in mind?

Suddenly, the first touch-paper is lit
By scurrying, shadowy figures.
A volley of cascading rainbows
Complains and screams its way skywards,
Followed by a deafening, defiant, silvery explosion;
A thousand glittering sparks expire,
As a gentle breeze wafts, ushering the drifting smoke east,
Clearing the stage for the next pyrotechnical display.
Is all this because of conspirators' plotting?

Then another and another and another,
Racing up from the ground
With a fierce, golden crackle, before exploding
Over the duck pond with a deafening, thunderous boom,
Forcing watching eyes to blink involuntarily.
Meanwhile, cold earth eats into numbed feet.
Familiar faces are all around us,
Their noses beginning to run in a sniff of protest.
This is a strange way to celebrate execution!

The whoosh and fizz of successive squibs,
Rockets spiralling their way upwards
Before exploding in a cacophonous roar,
As the crowd gasps its admiration.
Time and again, the volcanic action is repeated,
The rich, redolent smell of cordite, hanging in the air.
Less than an hour has elapsed.
It's all over for another year.
Remember, remember . . !

David Jasper

A Plea For Understanding

Forever on the outside, always looking in.
Feeling like a loser, never seem to win.
Other people living, as life was meant to be,
Happy friends together, oh why can't that be me?
I want to be accepted, I can't help being shy,
I long for understanding, before life passes by.
People are like flowers; some are bright and bold
And overshadow paler ones, leave them in the cold.
The pale ones have their beauty, not so obvious maybe,
But they blossom with attention, from those who care to see.

Ruth Ockendon Laycock

THE STEPPING STONE PATH

There's a stepping stone path by the River Tees,
Which leads from New Town End,
To a special place with boulders and trees,
Enclosing a sandy bay.

The amber Tees laps the pebble stones,
Which creep to the edge of the bay,
How many children must it have seen?
Whiling the hours away.

Countless children from far-off times,
And those children's children today,
And tomorrow's children not yet born,
Who will gather there to play.

And those couples who hand in hand have walked,
And laughed and talked this way,
Then lingered awhile at this special place,
Beside the sandy bay.

This special place has cast a spell,
On all who passed this way,
On all who trod the stepping stone path,
And stayed by the sandy bay.

But time will draw them back again,
In thoughts if not some way,
Once more they'll tread the stepping stone path,
Which leads to the sandy bay.

G Davies

RITUAL

Slice the bread and unbox the eggs.
Quarter a tomato and pierce the plastic
of an 'unhealthy' pack of bacon steaks.

Listen to the traffic coasting by
and listen to the birdsong. Imagine
you are anywhere but where you are:

in the kitchen chopping mushrooms
for your Sunday lunchtime fry-up.

The fridge freezer, now a regular
typecast character in your domestic
scratchings, whirrs into life and

you jump with a start. A neighbour
banging nails into a fence-post
hammers home the irony of day of rest.

Steve Urwin

LETTING GO

He is the only son of a single parent mum
Very close and beloved, around him her whole world spun
Now he is no longer small, a young man in his late teens
And the day has come when he'll find what being grown-up means.

They both worked hard, she earns their crust, he with his studies
So that one day he'll have his wish of going to university
At last his dream came true, and though pride showed in her eyes
He did not see the tears fall after they said their fond goodbyes.

Before, she didn't have the time to think or fret about tomorrow
She was too busy making plans and preparations to feel sorrow
But now, as she stood there watching the car speed out of sight
The full extent of this event brought home her lonely plight.

In all the years since he was born, he had her to depend on
She cared for him, shared in his joys, cheered him when he was down
Encouraged him through his ambitions so he would safeguard his future
Yet, never stopped to think, by letting go, she'll stand alone.

So now, she goes around the house, looking sadly at his belongings
With all she touches, her sobbing echoes round empty rooms
She knows now the raw pain of having to let go of her offspring
And the realisation that now he's independent, a young
                                                      man fully grown.

Hence, she must dry her tears and learn to look towards tomorrow
She has done all that she could to give her boy the life he chose
So now she owes it to herself to make a bright and happy future
Then she will feel no regrets, because she has learnt to let go.

M J Ellerton

DAISIES

I looked for happiness in my dreams,
but as I drew close,
I heard my soul whisper,
your happiness is a virgin born and
reared in the depths of your heart,
and when I opened up my heart to find her
I saw a candle, a cloak and a mirror
but happiness was not there.
I stayed a while and lit the candle
to contemplate where else to look.
It became cold in this heart,
and prompted by my despair
I wrapped the cloak of white day about me,
lined with the dark of night
her reason, a light in the darkness
her anger darkness amid the light,
and still happiness could not be found.
With time to spare I counted
every tear shed by sorrow
and found a river rushing by
and still happiness was not there.
A single thought threaded
a daisy chain through my hair,
I looked to the mirror
but my reflection was not there.
A silent whisper bid me close my eyes,
blinded without sight
I saw the fleeting ghost of love
stranded in a crystal ball of light
and I thought perchance
I could see happiness there.

And when the cold dawn of day awoke me
I took the daisies from my hair
wrapped my heart back up in my dreams
and put it away.

Aitch Brown

MEMORIES OF BOYHOOD

Sometimes I wander with my thoughts
Through silvan leafy vales;
The tracks I took when once a boy,
The woodlands and the dales.
Although my hair has now grown grey
The mists within my mind
Still conjure up a solace rare
Of youth and time in kind.

Once more my limbs are full of life,
The air like vintage wine;
I skirt the farmer's golden fields
With boyhood friends sublime.
We know each beech tree, every oak,
The willows by the stream,
The gap within the hedge, the spoor
Of footpads lie between.

Tumbling, tumbling down the slopes
Through matted grass and fern,
Our laughter echoes through the woods,
Before we reach the burn.
Gigantic ships on mighty rivers
Within our minds now grow:
Matchstick boats with captains, pirates,
Into whirlpools flow.

Cowboys, Indians, villains, heroes
Play on this verdant stage:
Camp fires burning, smoke is curling,
Round wigwams battles rage.
And when the chieftains call for peace,
The battle cry is o'er,
We gurgle water crystal clear
With bottled crumbs galore.

Librarian to the memory,
Sad be the vacant soul
Who now, midst archives past finds not
Some moments to recall.
A star amidst the night
Which down the corridors of life,
Bestoweth joy and light.

M Newble

THE TALE OF THE GHOST OF WHITE EMMA 1993

If you take the lane at the west end of the village
That leads to the cemetery beyond the school
Then take the narrow path
Past Gainford Wath
Around the corner lies Boat Pool

Go upstream from her dark brooding waters
Carry on through the bower of trees
To the grassy place
Where another wath's waters race
And Barforth Hall lies just over the Tees

To the left of the hall on the hillside
Stands a dovecot, and a chapel in ruins
From where the ghost of White Emma
Made village folk tremor
With its mysterious comings and goings

Fishermen in the dusk of the evening
And courting couples out late at night
Told of a banshee-like wailing
As down the hillside came sailing
Wreathed in mist, an object all white

Word spread round the village like wildfire
And no doubt the locals were scared
But one man, more brave than the rest,
Said that he'd do his best
To find out what it was if he dared

So one night he set out for the river
Along with a stout stick and his dog,
The breeze sighed through the trees
And the moon shone on the Tees
As he settled down to wait on a fallen tree log

He hadn't been there half an hour
When wailing broke the silence of the night
He felt cold, he felt hot
But was rooted to the spot
When into view came the object of white

Slowly it came down the hillside
Bealing and panting all the way to the brink
The dog didn't bother and the man realised
That there before his eyes
Was a white shorthorn bull stirk, taking a drink

Now old Walter Elland told me this story
And that leaves us in somewhat of a fix
Was it after his birth in 1892,
Or is it just legend or simply not true?
I think the secret died with him in 1966.

E D Bowen

Summer Fields

Velvet green with a silver hue
Beneath the summer skies of blue
A gentle sway beneath the breeze
Each blade of grass, it does tease
And through this carpet I do walk
Listening as the crickets talk
Breathing in the summer scent
Enjoying nature as it's meant
An aged oak stands very tall
And in its shadow I feel small
Taking comfort in its shade
Enjoying a glass of lemonade
Resting against the tree's coarse bark
Watching as day turns into dark
I ponder upon a day so right
And patiently await the morning light.

Andrea Parker

DEVOTION
(For Dave)

You ask me why do I love you
I love everything about you and all that is you
You are kind, gentle, loving and caring
Above all a wonderful man

My darling do not doubt the love I have for you
Be assured my feelings run deep
Deep enough to touch my heart, my soul, my very being
Let nothing put doubt in your mind, trust in my promises
Believe me as I pledge my heart to you
Rest in the comfort and peace that is our love

Life is too short for doubts and questions
From birth to leaving this earth is fleeting
To share that time with a true love with you is a gift
We are all individuals with our own special qualities
Trust me when I say you are the special man for me
I do not give my love lightly I am devoted to you.

Carolyn Horner

SUBMISSIONS INVITED
SOMETHING FOR EVERYONE

POETRY NOW 2003 - Any subject, any style, any time.

WOMENSWORDS 2003 - Strictly women, have your say the female way!

STRONGWORDS 2003 - Warning! Age restriction, must be between 16-24, opinionated and have strong views.
(Not for the faint-hearted)

All poems no longer than 30 lines.
Always welcome! No fee!
Cash Prizes to be won!

Mark your envelope (eg *Poetry Now*) **2003**
Send to:
Forward Press Ltd
Remus House, Coltsfoot Drive,
Peterborough, PE2 9JX

OVER £10,000 POETRY PRIZES TO BE WON!

Judging will take place in October 2003